Caring for the Physical and Mental Health of People with Learning Disabilities

of related interest

Group Homes for People with Intellectual Disabilities
Encouraging Inclusion and Participation
Tim Clement and Christine Bigby
Foreword by Professor Jim Mansell
ISBN 978 1 84310 645 6

Living with Learning Disabilities, Dying with Cancer
Thirteen Personal Stories
Irene Tuffrey-Wijne
Foreword by Sheila Hollins
ISBN 978 1 84905 027 2

Understanding Intensive Interaction
Context and Concepts for Professionals and Families
Graham Firth, Ruth Berry and Cath Irvine
ISBN 978 1 84310 982 2

Bereavement, Loss and Learning Disabilities
A Guide for Professionals and Carers
Robin Grey
ISBN 978 1 84905 020 3

Activities for Adults with Learning Disabilities
Having Fun, Meeting Needs
Helen Sonnet and Ann Taylor
ISBN 978 1 84310 975 4

Authentic Dialogue with People who are Developmentally Disabled
Sad without Tears
Jennifer Hill
ISBN 978 1 84905 016 6

Health Care and the Autism Spectrum
A Guide for Health Professionals, Parents and Carers
Alison Morton-Cooper
ISBN 978 1 85302 963 9

Caring for the Physical and Mental Health of People with Learning Disabilities

David Perry, Louise Hammond, Geoff Marston,
Sherryl Gaskell and James Eva

Foreword by Dr Anthony Kearns

Jessica Kingsley *Publishers*
London and Philadelphia

First published in 2011
by Jessica Kingsley Publishers
116 Pentonville Road
London N1 9JB, UK
and
400 Market Street, Suite 400
Philadelphia, PA 19106, USA

www.jkp.com

Library of Congress Cataloging in Publication Data
Caring for the physical and mental health of people with learning
disabilities / David Perry ... [et. al.] ; foreword by Anthony Kearns.
    p. cm.
Includes bibliographical references and index.
ISBN 978-1-84905-131-6 (alk. paper)
1. Learning disabled--Medical care. 2. Learning
disabled--Mental health. I. Perry, David.
RC394.L37C37 2010
362.196'85889--dc22
                                        2010016831

British Library Cataloguing in Publication Data
A CIP catalogue record for this book is available from the British Library

ISBN 978 1 84905 131 6

Printed and bound in Great Britain by
MPG Books Group

Contents

Foreword

Before writing this introduction I had to deliver an introductory lecture as in-service training to a group of staff of varying experience, from unqualified care staff to psychologists and teachers. A member of the audience told me afterwards that he was a little nonplussed by one of my comments. I had referred to some item as probably to be found in the textbooks. He explained that, as a carer without formal qualifications, he never had a straightforward reference work. He was delighted to hear that someone had written the kind of text he needed. Similarly gratifying reactions have come from others to whom I have mentioned the idea. This experience reinforced my pleasure at being asked to write this foreword.

In many settings working with people with learning disability over the years I have been concerned to see how little basic grounding is given to staff about the health care needs of the people with whom they work. Certainly, they may be provided with instruction as to the practical aspects of providing care and some information about the legal and ethical issues; however, this information is often very selective and pertains mainly to the particular organisation. In the real world, also, notes taken at any induction tend to be mislaid. Government reviews, such as *Putting People First* and *Valuing People Now*, have reviewed the deficits in service provision for people with learning disability and how they can and must be addressed. Special areas of need have been considered, such as autistic spectrum disorders. There has been much focus on the rights of the person with a learning disability to make choices in all areas of their life and to have help with making these when necessary.

What has been needed is a short, non-technical text to give carers (and others who require an aide-memoire) a single easily accessible source of reference. In this textbook its experienced authors have admirably achieved this goal.

Dr Anthony Kearns FRCPsych
Consultant Forensic Psychiatrist in Learning Disability
Royston, Herts, March 2010

The Physical Health and Mental Health Needs of People with a Learning Disability

Chapter 1

About This Book

In the past 25 years there has been significant change in the way people with learning disabilities are cared for in the United Kingdom and many other parts of the world. Following the closure of long-stay residential hospitals in many parts of the world, people with learning disabilities have returned to live in community settings. This has borne fruit in terms of many advantages relating to improved accommodation, work and leisure and opportunities, thus enabling more rewarding and fulfilling lives for these people. However, it has become increasingly apparent that some physical and psychological needs are not being satisfactorily met, and frequently this is because such needs are not detected, or acted upon, in a timely manner.

When people with learning disabilities lived in the confines of large residential hospitals they were under 24-hour supervision by qualified nursing staff, and the 'care' of doctors. For many people with learning disabilities this was unnecessary, and often the physical conditions in which they lived were poor. However, staff developed a degree of expertise in assessing and managing both physical and psychiatric illnesses in their clients.

Following closure of the hospitals, and the move into community residential provision, staffing arrangements changed. People with learning disabilities were now looked after by care staff with vocational qualifications, and their medical needs were met by local general practitioners (GPs).

Currently in the UK, medical schools devote little time to training students about the specific health-care needs of people with learning disabilities, usually no more than one or two days in a five-year course. Furthermore, many GPs have few such patients on their books. Not surprisingly, therefore, their knowledge in this area is often scant, particularly with respect to the health issues related to specific genetic syndromes.

Difficulties in this area are compounded by the ways in which doctors are taught to diagnose. Traditionally, this has been done by taking a history of an illness, carrying out a physical examination, and then, if necessary, arranging special investigations, such as blood tests or various scans. Unfortunately, people with learning disabilities, particularly those with more severe degrees, do not neatly fit this model. Often they have problems that do not have a simple or easily understood history. Sometimes they resist physical examination, and are frightened and disturbed by physical investigations like blood tests or scans.

This often means that physical health problems are unidentified until they have progressed to a late stage. Successful treatment may then prove more difficult, with poorer outcomes as a result. This is particularly true of non-verbal clients, who may only respond to pain or distress with disturbed behaviour.

It is more recognised today that psychiatric disorders present in atypical ways in people with learning disabilities, and that this can lead to delays in diagnosis. Illness is often misunderstood, and erroneously attributed to other reasons. This is particularly sad considering the fact that people with learning disabilities are at as much as two and a half times the general risk of a wide range of physical health problems.

Who is this book for?

This book is intended to be useful for the following groups of people.

Family or paid carers

Family members or paid carers may be in a position where they need to:

- support a person with learning disabilities to access services by attending appointments with them, and providing accurate information about health matters

- prepare a person to access services, e.g. by taking them for a preparatory visit

- monitor health outcomes, e.g. by weighing a person who is dieting or on certain medications, or monitoring blood sugars (if a person is diabetic)

- liaise with specialist professionals to ensure the person's health needs are met.

This support might also be described as 'health facilitation' – ensuring that the health needs of the person are represented and met.

Professional health facilitators

This group includes community nurses and social workers who have a wider remit, including the following:

- work with people with learning disabilities and carers to discover their experiences of primary health care, with a view to contributing to future service developments

- set up, administer and monitor annual health checks

- assist paid and unpaid carers in providing up-to-date, useful and evidence-based information on personal health needs

- update the knowledge-base and skills of members of the Primary Health Care Team, including GPs

- assist with the continuing identification of people with learning disabilities

- encourage general practitioners to use a standardised computer code on their information systems so that patients with a learning disability can be easily identified. (This would be useful for identifying people for particular screening programmes, e.g. Down's syndrome.)

- assist with good health promotion, particularly amongst people from minority ethnic groups

- act as route for information between Primary Health Care Trusts, specialist services (e.g. consultant learning disability psychiatrists or psychologists) and clients/carers

- provide quality information to commisioners so better services can be developed.

For the purposes of this book, we will simply use the term 'carers' throughout, unless sections are written specifically for one group or the other (and in those cases, we will make this explicit). A glossary at the end of the book provides an explanation of all technical terms.

Why is support required?

People with learning disabilities are at much greater risk of physical and psychiatric illness than the population at large – some estimates suggest up to two and a half times the general risk. The chapters that follow list the common health problems that arise, along with information about their relationship with learning disability and advice on how to support those who experience them.

These problems may be related to, or resulting from, the underlying cause of the learning disability – e.g. Down's syndrome is often associated with thyroid or heart disease, tuberous sclerosis and epilepsy. Others may be related to lifestyle circumstances, e.g. lack of exercise and poor dietary intake, which contribute to the likelihood of having problems associated with obesity, diabetes or cerebrovascular disease.

The following difficulties are commonly found in relation to the illness of people with learning disabilities:

- People with learning disabilities have difficulty accessing primary care.
- Carers may not recognise health needs, or the presence of illness.
- There is poor uptake by such people of screening programmes, e.g. cervical cytology.
- There is over-reliance on psychotropic drugs for the management of challenging behaviour.
- Health outcomes for people with learning disabilities fall far short of expectations for the general population.
- People with learning disabilities have a reduced life expectancy of approximately ten years.

Carers not only need to overcome the problems of higher rates of illness and difficulties of initial identification of such illness, but also face difficulties in dealing with staff who may have limited experience in dealing with people with a learning disability, and access to primary (general practitioner) and secondary (hospital) care.

Table 1.1 gives a range of practical tips suggesting steps that can be taken by a carer acting as a health facilitator to ensure that access to, and experience of, health care for the person for whom they care is improved.

Table 1.1 How to overcome barriers to obtaining health care

Situation	Advice
When a hospital is unaware that a patient has a learning disability	Ensure the GP clearly identifies the fact in their referral letter. Also, that they detail any problems which may follow from this (e.g. consent/capacity, behavioural problems).
For a person with communication problems e.g. the patient is non-verbal	Request a 'double' appointment to account for the fact that communication will be slower.
	Ensure someone accompanies the patient who knows the background to the problem.
	Take a written history from the staff team.
	Use communication aids, e.g. 'books without words' or a communication dictionary.
When the patient becomes distressed whilst waiting	Ask for the first appointment of the day.
	Ask for a home visit (hospital consultants can visit at home if a GP requests it).
	Arrange a preparatory visit to enable familiarisation with environment.
	Take enough help – whether staff or relatives – to contain a challenging situation.
	Consider sedation prior to a hospital visit – anaesthetic in extreme circumstances.
Problems with long waiting lists	Consider private medicine, if finances are available.
	Approach your local patient advisory service. Talk to the person's GP about approaching another trust or service.

Chapter 2

An Introduction to Learning Disabilities

What are learning disabilities?

In the UK, the term 'learning disability' (LD) is used to describe people who have a significant impairment of intellectual ability, with the need for additional help to live independently. In other countries other terms are used, such as 'intellectual disability' or 'mental retardation'. However, all these terms refer to the same broad problems.

The definition of LD was originally statistically driven, given that (like height) intelligence is distributed normally across the population, with an average IQ of approximately 100. Most people fall within a range of 80 and 120, but (as with height) some people fall significantly below 80, while others are above 120. Those individuals whose IQ is less than 70 (about 2.5 per cent of the population) are said to have a learning disability. The level of LD is further divided into those with 'mild', 'moderate' or 'severe' LD. Most fall in the mild range.

Currently, the use of IQ testing is decreasing, because it is recognised that assessing a person's adaptive intelligence and level of functioning based on their overall history (including developmental milestones as an infant, educational abilities and achievements, employment history, communication, social, economic and other aspects of life) is far more important than a single test of isolated cognitive skills when making a decision as to whether or not there is an LD and how severe it is. There are further problems with IQ testing that also reduce its reliability. These include:

- which test is used
- who is administering the test (different assessors may score things differently, depending on their skills)
- which language the test is in (e.g. if the person being assessed has a language other than English as their native language, it can affect their score)
- how many times the same test has been done with that person (people can improve their scores with practice)
- the effects of sensory deficits (e.g. poor hearing, visual defects)
- the effects of additional mental disorders (e.g. depression, psychosis, anxiety)
- the side-effects of some medications (e.g. drowsiness).

In spite of the clear limitations in respect of reliability of IQ testing as a diagnostic tool, IQ tests do have some relevance for assessing the possible progression or worsening of a person's cognitive functions over time. So, for example, having an IQ score in a person's records is useful when, in the future, further problems occur. Re-testing can provide a basis for comparison. In some people with LD (e.g. Down's syndrome and some metabolic disorders) there is a risk of a further deterioration in abilities occurring, and serial IQ testing can help to measure this.

Although IQ testing is not a precise or reliable science, we have to have some way of differentiating different people with LD according to the severity of their disorder. This is because we need a common language or terms of reference for both legal and administrative purposes – e.g. to determine whether a person should be prosecuted for an offence, or whether they are entitled to a particular service or benefit. Full biographical descriptions of each person's abilities, or lack thereof, are too bulky and unwieldy for these narrow purposes.

Finally, IQ testing can raise suspicions about specific and particular cognitive problems (e.g. dyslexia or specific reading problems, memory problems, calculation problems or organisational problems), and this can inform therapists and carers about particular areas of need or support requirements.

Most definitions of LD not only emphasise cognitive problems leading to reduced abilities to solve problems or communicate, but also that people need extra help to live independently, to be able to solve problems in day-to-day life situations. Such definitions also cover the fact that these problems start early in life, usually before the age of 18. This is because people can still develop symptoms that share many characteristics with learning disabilities after this point, and may appear to have LD (for example, due to a head injury or a severe mental illness). Although people suffering from these can superficially (or, sometimes, overtly) appear similar to people with LD, such people are not included in the definitions that we are using within this book.

Assessing different levels of learning disability

Learning disability is further defined according to different levels of 'deficit'. The majority of people with LD have a 'mild' degree, which is traditionally set between IQ scores of 50 and 69 (though, as mentioned above, beware of the limitations of relying solely upon an IQ test assessment). 'Moderate' LD describes people who have an IQ test score of between 35 and 49, and 'severe' and 'profound' is usually used to describe people whose IQ is assessed as being below 34 and 20 respectively. Table 2.1 summarises the different levels of LD in relation to adaptive functioning. 'Adaptive functioning' is the relative ability, or disability, of a person to carry out the activities of daily living – from the most simple things, such as washing or dressing, right through to carrying out complicated tasks.

Table 2.1 Severity of learning disability

Areas of ability	Mild LD (IQ 69–50)	Moderate LD (IQ 49–35)	Severe/ Profound LD (IQ 34–0)
Expressive language	Delayed, but everyday speech useful	Delayed, and uses simple phrases only	Severe delay, with few words or absent speech
Comprehension	Reasonable	Limited to simple phrases/requests	Very limited understanding, if any
Non-verbal communication	Good	Limited	Rudimentary
Self-care	Fully independent in washing, eating, dressing. Normal continence	Limited achievements; supervision may be required. Mainly continent	Very limited. Supervision always required. Mainly incontinent
Independent living	Possible	Needs some supervision	24-hour supervision required
Academic work	Experiences difficulties, but should learn to read, write and do simple maths	Limited achievements. May develop some reading, writing and maths skills	Some simple visuo-spatial skills
Employment	Capable of work demanding practical rather than academic skills	Simple practical work with supervision	Most not capable of this
Mobility	Normal	Delayed, but usually fully mobile	Frequent musculo-skeletal abnormalities. Often severely restricted
Social development	Some immaturity, but otherwise normal	Limited, but usually can interact	May be very limited. Autism common
Associated deficits	As normal population	Some increase in Central Nervous System disorders, e.g. epilepsy	Frequent Central Nervous System disorders. Often have epilepsy, and sensory deficits

(*source*: Geoff Marston)

Assessments that establish different levels of learning disability enable carers and professionals to understand better the needs of a particular person with learning disability.

Causes of learning disability

There are literally hundreds of different disorders that result in LD. These can include those arising from pre-conception issues with the mother or father, and go on right through to events occurring in late childhood (up to 18 years).

Why is it useful to know the cause of the learning disability?

It is important, if possible, to determine *why* someone has an LD because doing so can help to predict what may be expected to happen in future, and can help professionals and carers to plan what services and assistance that person with LD may require. It can also help predict the type of associated physical problems that are more likely to arise, and thus assist services in planning interventions (e.g. with Down's syndrome, heart valve surgery may be required at some stage).

However, in many people with mild to moderate LD the cause is never known, although advances in genetics and other fields are continually shedding light in cases where the causes were previously unknown. Generally speaking, mild LD cases are not associated with significant health issues, apart from high levels of obesity (which is discussed later in this book) and a reduced uptake of preventative health strategies, such as health-screening programmes.

In most severe LD cases there is an identified cause, most commonly a genetic one. This is a complex subject, but it is very important to have a basic understanding of it, because it determines so much of the other, associated problems that may arise. (In the Appendix at the end of the book there is a brief description of genetic causes of learning disabilities.)

Environmental causes of learning disability

In Table 2.2 there are examples given of some of the more common causes of LD, although there are also many others. If you find any of the terminology in Table 2.2 unfamiliar, do turn to the glossary provided at the end of this book.

Table 2.2 Some known causes of learning disability

Age	Cause
Before conception	• Maternal exposure to radiation or chemicals • Genetic/Chromosomal disorders
0–9 months (prenatal)	• Infection of foetus during pregnancy due to toxoplasma, rubella, cytomegalovirus, herpes, or syphilis • Trauma during pregnancy (e.g. road traffic accident)
At birth	• Premature birth • Hypoxia (e.g. placenta praevia, cord around neck, severe anaemia) • Jaundice ('kernicterus') • Traumatic birth
Neonatal period	• Dehydration • Infection – e.g. due to pneumonia, meningitis • Trauma
Infancy	• Infection – e.g. due to meningitis, encephalitis arising from measles or other infective agents • Trauma • Brain tumours • Hydrocephaly • Some forms of epilepsy • Cerebral malaria • Non-accidental injury • Nutritional, e.g. iodine deficiency, leading to hypothyroidism and 'cretinism'
Childhood	• Trauma (e.g. road traffic accident) • Non-accidental injury • Metabolic disorders (e.g. glycogen storage diseases) • Nutritional deficiency (e.g. iodine deficiency), leading to hypothyroidism and 'cretinism'

Genetic causes of learning disability

Some LDs are genetic in origin, but it is difficult to know exactly what percentage of people have this as a cause. Proportions around the world will differ due to the different environmental influences present (e.g. the environmental cause of neonatal dehydration is common in many countries, but not in developed countries).

Because this is a more complex area to understand than some others covered in this book, we provide below an overview of what this term actually means in a practical sense. A more detailed explanation of genetics and its relation to learning disability can be found in the Appendix to this book on page 143.

Genetics refers to the way in which our own body 'make up' influences our physical, intellectual and mental/personality development. Parents pass on key 'genetic' information within their egg and sperm to enable the few cells of the foetus to grow into a baby, then into a child and adult. This genetic influence on development is independent of the environment we grow up in and any trauma that might be faced during life. However, sometimes toxic substances (e.g. radiation and certain chemicals) can affect the genetic material held in the sperm/eggs of the parents and this can then affect the child.

There are many genetic disorders (3,000 plus) and nearly 40 per cent of these are associated with a learning disability. Each type of disorder will influence a person's physical and mental health in a different way. For this reason it is important to try and identify the type of disorder, where possible, in order to understand better that person's physical health needs and to plan for their future – see the Appendix to this book. For fuller details of specific disorders we suggest that the Contact a Family directory (www.cafamily.org.uk) is a useful resource.

Chapter 3
Learning Disabilities and Physical Health

This chapter will look at those health issues which are most amenable to lifestyle changes rather than medical treatment. These include obesity, constipation and urinary problems. It also aims to give guidance on how physical illness might be detected in someone with a learning disability and poor communication skills.

Below are listed some of the more common physical health problems associated with learning disability:

- constipation
- dental health problems
- epilepsy
- heart disease
- hypertension
- incontinence (urinary more common than faecal)
- mental illness
- obesity
- sensory impairment

- skin disease

- thyroid disease.

- upper digestive tract problems.

Recognising physical illness in someone with a learning disability

When a person with a learning disability feels unwell, they may try to seek help and, depending on their own perception of the seriousness of their condition. They may use different sources of help, such as asking friends or relatives for advice, buying medicines from a chemist, shop or supermarket, visiting a doctor or calling an ambulance. In doing so, they are interpreting their own symptoms to a degree, on the basis of symptom type – whether it be pain, nausea, etc. – its severity and the speed of onset, deciding how quickly they need help, and what kind of help that should be.

For most of us this process of seeking help is fairly obvious and forms part of regular daily life. However, the ability of people with learning disabilities to carry out such a decision-making process may be impaired. In those with a more severe disability, others may need to make the necessary decisions. This is one reason why, particularly for those with more severe disability, physical illness is often detected at a relatively late stage in people with learning disabilities.

One metaphor for the human body could be that of a car, consisting of a number of sub-systems linked together. When a car breaks down the mechanic begins by trying to ascertain the cause. It could be a fuel problem, an electrical fault or something mechanical such as a broken cam-belt. Any of these separate problems could be the cause of the engine breakdown. In the same way, symptoms or signs of illness that a person with learning disabilities displays, or complains of, might indicate a fault in a specific bodily system, but could also be caused by a wide variety of other problems.

An example would be chest pain, which can be due to a variety of different problems such as an injury to the chest wall or to internal organs such as heart and lungs. For example, it could arise from inflammation of the heart lining/pericarditis; heart attack/myocardial infarction; lung infection/pneumonia; or inflammation of the lung lining/pleurisy. Problems with the upper gastro-intestinal tract, such as oesophagitis/inflammation of the oesophagus and acid reflux/heartburn, can also present with chest pain. So can problems of the chest wall, such as fractured ribs or inflammation of joints in the rib cage or thoracic (upper) spine.

Below, we provide a summary of a likely sequence of events when a person with a learning disability visits a doctor with a physical complaint.

- A doctor presented with a person with learning disability with a physical complaint has first to decide which 'system' is involved. The resulting investigation and treatments will then vary widely. The doctor will attempt to make an initial differential diagnosis by taking a history of the symptom(s), such as pain, how long it has been present, what makes it come on, what makes it go away, what it feels like, where exactly it is (e.g. within the chest), etc., and details of any other symptoms that may accompany the main one. This may give further clues to the cause.

- The carer's or relative's opinion of the problem can be very helpful. Sometimes a person's behaviour will suggest pain – e.g. a screwed-up face; banging ears in a way that suggests they may have earache; rubbing their chest after a meal or drink, which might point to acid reflux.

- The doctor then carries out a physical examination, and, if necessary, conducts some basic investigations. This is a process doctors learn in medical school. However, with someone who cannot communicate, or may actively resist physical examination (particularly people with conditions such as autism) the steps to diagnosis may prove difficult to carry out.

Key symptoms to look out for and how to respond

It is not just useful, but can be life-saving for a carer to be aware of physical illness at an early stage. Table 3.1 lists symptoms and signs that suggest particular problems affecting certain physical systems.

Table 3.1 Signs suggesting physical-health problems

Nature of the problem	Symptoms
Medication-related	• Dizziness/unsteadiness • Rash • Sleepiness
Heart-related	• Chest pains on exercise (angina), sometimes radiating to neck and arm • Shortness of breath (especially when exercising) • Problem sleeping (especially lying flat) • Blue lips or extremities • Swollen ankles
Lung-related	• Chest pain, worse on breathing/coughing • Persistent cough • Phlegm production • Wheezing or noisy breathing • Shortness of breath • Increased breathing rate, i.e. more than 20 breaths a minute
Gastro-intestinal	• Prolonged vomiting • Vomiting blood or altered blood (coffee-ground vomit) • Change in bowel habit • Weight loss • Passing blood or mucus in stools
Urinary tract	• Frequency of urination increases • Burning on urination • Onset of incontinence • Blood in urine • Getting up at night to pass urine • Poor flow of urine • Apparent pain on passing urine
Joints and connective tissue	• Swelling/pain in joints • Reduced range of movement • Red, hot joints

Blood-related	• Swollen glands
	• Pale
	• Lacking energy
	• Breathless
Glands	• Weight gain or weight loss
	• Anxiety, tremor (thyrotoxic)
	• Lethargy, lacking energy (hypothyroid)
	• Other – depends on which 'glands'

Below is a list of situations in which serious warning signs suggest that immediate medical attention is required. If the person:

- is unconscious
- is bleeding heavily
- has an obvious or suspected broken bone
- has a deep laceration
- has chest pain
- is having difficulty breathing.

If you identify any of the above symptoms, seek medical attention immediately.

Physical health, nutrition and exercise

One significant way in which a carer can support the physical health needs of the person with a learning disability is to understand the cause of their particular disability and to enable them to have a lifestyle that encourages good health.

Constipation

Constipation is a very common problem that is particularly associated with people with more severe degrees of learning disability. It is a condition that can be associated with distress, disturbed behaviour and worsening of other conditions, such as epilepsy.

There are many reasons why people with learning disabilities are so prone to the condition. In some cases it is because there are abnormalities in the nervous system that controls movement of food through the bowels. This is often complicated by what people eat, by their low fluid intake and by their lack of physical activity. In others, constipation can be a sign of a serious underlying physical illness, particularly if it is a new problem, and in this case should be given further assessment.

Examples of conditions causing constipation include partial blockage of the bowels due to tumours, metabolic disorders affecting calcium metabolism and an under-active thyroid gland.

Below is a list of measures you can take to help someone reduce constipation where there is not a specific and serious cause for it:

- Ensure the diet contains adequate fibre. In the first place this can be done by including additional fruit and vegetables and wholemeal bread.

- Try to increase fluid intake up to 3 litres per day if possible (avoid tea and coffee as this tends to dehydrate people).

- Encourage exercise.

- If laxatives are required, be aware of the way in which they work. Some, such as senna, should not be used in the long term because they work by acting as an irritant to the lining of the bowel and may cause diarrhoea and abdominal cramps. Bulking agents or softening preparations are a better first step ; these are often made from ispaghula husks, e.g. Fybogel® or Movicol®.

- If someone has chronic constipation, seek specialist advice seek specialist advice from a gastroenterologist, as other treatments may be required. A combination of different remedies may be successful. In a very small minority, enemas on a regular basis may be needed These are usually administered by nurses attached to the Primary Health Care team.

Incontinence

Urinary incontinence is also known as 'involuntary micturation' (urination). This normally affects is around 10 per cent of the general female population, but it is probably much higher in older age groups.

Incontinence is of many types, such as 'stress incontinence' (e.g. which occur when coughing), urge incontinence ('when you have to go, you have to go') and continuous, like 'water over the edge of a dam' – see Table 3.2. Often people with LD with severe disability have never been continent, usually because a toileting programme has never been implemented or successfully completed.

People caring for an incontinent person need to be aware that wearing incontinence pads increases the risk of urinary tract infections (UTI). At night it is better for an individual to lie on a protective sheet, such as a 'Kylie', in order to allow air to circulate. It is also essential that a high level of hygiene is maintained, with thorough washing and drying of the genital region, and ensuring in females that, if they are faecally incontinent, they wipe or are wiped from front to back to prevent spreading germs. The application of barrier creams can help to maintain skin integrity (good skin), but should not be used on skin that has broken down (rashes, sores, etc.), unless directed by a doctor.

If the person has always been continent, and then becomes incontinent, a visit to their doctor is advised, and it is helpful if a sample can be taken from the first urine of the day for urinalysis (urine testing).

The doctor will ask questions such as:

- Is the person in pain?
- Is the person experiencing a burning sensation?
- Is the urine dark in colour and foul-smelling?
- Is the flow of urine continuous or interrupted?
- Is the person urinating frequently through the night?
- Is there an increase in the amount of fluid being drunk?
- They might also ask: Is there any itching of the genitals?

The reason for asking these questions is to rule out symptoms of diabetes, or of UTI. The urine will be tested for infection and diabetes at the surgery, and, if required, sent for further testing, including microbiology, culture and antibiotic sensitivity (MC&S).

Table 3.2 Quick reference guide to urinary incontinence

	Stress Pattern	Urge Pattern	Overflow Pattern	Notes
Stress incontinence	Yes	No	No	Urine collection poses difficulties for many people. The use of conventional collecting kits/pots can be offputting as the toilet looks different. Alternative methods that may be implemented include cling film placed loosely in the toilet
UTI	No	Yes	Yes	
Bladder instability *	No	Yes	No	
Overflow obstruction	Possible	No	Yes	
Prosta-tectomy	Possible	Yes	No	Prostate Questions of urine flow, speed and pattern need to be addressed. It can often be difficult to gain clear, concise information regarding this, so use questions such as: • 'Do you still want to "wee" when you have just been?' • Do carers observe frequent repeated visits? A practical example for alternative methods of presenting information include: • Using a tap to demonstrate steady urine stream, or stop/start motion is a helpful way to gain information in relation to whether further examination or PSA blood tests may be required.

*also known as detrusor instability, characterised by spontaneous and uninhibited contraction of the bladder muscle during bladder filling. The bladder pressure exceeds the urethral pressure, resulting in incontinence.

Obesity

Obesity (being significantly over-weight) is now recognised as being a major health problem in people with LD, of whom up to 40 per cent suffer with the condition. The reasons for it are multi-factorial.

There are some particular syndromes associated with learning disabilities that are associated with over-eating. An example is Prader-Willi syndrome, a chromosomal disorder that leads to dramatic over-eating, severe obesity and, if untreated, early death. This is quite rare and is today usually diagnosed in childhood.

Down's syndrome is a more common condition associated with obesity, and in this condition an under-active thyroid gland (hypothyroidism) can be the cause. Consequently, if you are caring for someone with Down's syndrome who starts putting on weight for no apparent reason, it is prudent to ask their general practitioner to perform thyroid function tests.

WHY WORRY ABOUT OBESITY?

There are many people walking around who appear to be over-weight, but seem to be healthy. The reason for concern is that being significantly over-weight is associated not only with reduced mobility and quality of life, but also with a number of serious medical conditions. These include increased risk of:

- diabetes – which itself can give rise to problems of poor control of sugar levels in blood, leading to hyperglycaemia (high blood sugar), which not only has serious effects in itself, but can also lead to kidney disease and, ultimately, kidney failure

- peripheral vascular problems

- an increase in some cancers

- high blood pressure

- heart attacks

- strokes

- osteoarthritis, due to excess weight on joints.

Considering the benefits of losing weight on one's future health, it is important that this should be a priority in people with LD who are obese.

HOW TO DETERMINE WHETHER OR NOT SOMEONE IS OBESE

Given the fact that many people with LD are relatively short in stature, we try to work out their 'Body Mass Index' (BMI). This is a formula that takes height into consideration when determining if someone is over-weight. To calculate BMI, height is measured in metres, then squared, and divided by the person's weight in kilograms.

$$BMI = \frac{(height\ in\ metres)^2}{(weight\ in\ kilograms)}$$

A Body Mass Index between 25 and 30 means the person is over-weight and should make attempts to lose weight. If the BMI is over 30, this is serious, and significant problems exist. Such people need medical assessment and the assistance of a dietician.

REASONS FOR OBESITY

In most people there is no underlying medical cause for being over-weight. There are some rare endocrine (gland) problems that can cause people to be obese, but in the majority of cases it is simply because energy intake is greater than energy expenditure. Even a minimal increase of calorie intake of as little as 100 per day (one packet of crisps or a small bar of chocolate, over several months, will lead to a small, steady increase in weight. Consequently, even a modest reduction in intake will reverse matters, and lead to slow, steady weight loss.

In people with LD, the most common cause of weight gain is a diet too rich in fats and/or carbohydrates (high calorific content), made worse by insufficient physical activity. In most cases fairly over-weight people can achieve weight loss without specialist helps but crash-diets are not useful in the long term. Ideally, the aim should be to achieve weight loss of no more than 1 kilogram per week. This can be done in a number of simple ways:

1. First, reduce the amount of refined sugar in the diet. This is often hidden in such foods as cakes and biscuits.

2. Next, reduce the amount of fatty foods, such as cheese, full-fat milk, butter, eggs and fatty meats.

These two measures alone, particularly if combined with minimal exercise, such as regular walks, swimming, etc., can lead to a degree of weight loss. However, if someone has a more significant weight problem (a BMI greater than 30), then it may be necessary to ask for help before starting them on a weight-loss programme. Depending on the age of the person, and how long they have been over-weight, a medical examination may be appropriate to determine whether the obesity has led to any other health problems, such as hypertension, diabetes or high blood cholesterol. Tests can usually be carried out by the GP, and, if necessary, specific treatment for any related problems can be given.

The help of a dietician may be required, to draw up a sensible dietary programme, and give advice about safe exercise. Fad diets are best avoided in people with LD. Their dietary intake needs to be modified over a longer period, rather than attempting to achieve rapid weight loss over a short time, for purposes such as 'going on holiday'.

It should also be borne in mind that the majority of the general population have problems losing weight! The willingness and cooperation of the person involved is necessary, and, if at all possible, their agreement must be sought before dietary restrictions are arbitrarily placed on them. (We look at this in more detail later in the chapter.)

Carers should try to avoid becoming involved in conflicts with people who do not want to change their eating habits. If a carer becomes 'obsessed' about what people eat, this can trigger an anorexia-style condition. It must also be remembered that some people can be both obese and malnourished at the same time. This is a particular risk in people with autism who can develop food fads, becoming very focused or driven by one type of food. This can be the only thing they will eat and are often things such as potato crisps or ice cream. Consequently if this becomes a long standing habit then malnourishment and vitamin deficiencies can occur, requiring the input of a dietician and the need for supplementation. Some people with LD are vegetarian, and, if they make that choice, they should be advised as to what types of vegetables, cereals and fruit, etc. they will need in order to maintain adequate nutritional intake. This type of help can be provided by dieticians.

Supporting people's diet, well-being and exercise

The food we eat and the type and amount of exercise we take have a direct influence on our health and general well-being. The human body requires food to build tissues and to create the energy needed to maintain breathing, circulation, digestion, growth and repair. Even after reaching adulthood, our entire bodies are continually replaced, cell by cell, over a period of approximately seven years.

It is accepted nowadays that there is a relationship between high levels of heart disease in Western countries and modern diets, which contain excessive levels of processed foods that are high in fat, salt and sugar, and low in fibre content.

The right food

It is important to try to eat high-quality food for body maintenance, which is made up of a balance of proteins, fats, carbohydrates, vitamins, minerals, trace elements and water. When combined with exercise to ensure a reasonable level of fitness, this will help achieve a healthy body, high levels of energy and a general sense of confidence and vitality. A sensible healthy diet need not be monotonous or restricting, or deprive anyone of their favourite foods for ever.

For people with learning disability, these areas are often overlooked. However, a moderate and balanced diet of both the right quality and variety of foods would promote good health and assist mental and physical well-being, enabling people with learning disability to get the most out of life.

Many people with learning disability have unhealthy or inappropriate diets, leading, as mentioned above, to a high prevalence of obesity. There are many reasons for this. Many people with learning disabilities are living more independently than before with obvious benefits to them, but their dietary intake often suffers, with increased numbers of people eating takeaway food or pre-prepared microwave meals. A healthy eating programme for people with learning disabilities who are living independently is likely to lead to a noticeable improvement in their appearance, with improved skin and hair condition, and greater levels of energy and vitality.

The dangers of severe dieting

It is not wise to change people's eating habits overnight, even if they are over-weight. It is not a good idea to go on a severe slimming diet that severely reduces calorie intake, as this merely puts the body on 'starvation alert'. The concept of many weight-loss diets is that of reducing the total calorie intake per day until it is less than the amount of calories used by the body as fuel. The theory is that the body will get some of its energy by breaking down fat stored in the tissues, thus causing weight loss. This may seem logical, but some studies suggest that vital bodily processes will react to a deliberate reduction of calories in the same way as they react in times of famine. If the body is 'tricked' into a 'famine mode', it will adopt survival techniques. These include lowering the metabolic rate so as not to use up fat reserves quickly, and, at the first opportunity, when food is more abundant (or when dieting stops), it will overcompensate by storing up even more fat than before, in case of a future famine. The result can be a vicious circle of dieting, weight loss and additional weight gain, which is impossible to break until a sensible eating plan is adopted.

Tips to encourage healthy eating

The easiest and most beneficial way to change eating habits is to gradually replace the most undesirable types of food in the diet with healthy alternatives. Here are some suggestions:

- It is easier to continue with a healthy eating plan if the person is not continually hungry: always have fruit and even raw vegetables to prevent this empty feeling. Fruit is a good 'filler', full of fibre, water, carbohydrates and vitamins. Eating this can help prevent snacking between meals on carbohydrate or fat-rich sweets, chocolates, cakes, etc., or even apparently 'healthy' cereal bars (which actually contain sugar and hidden calories).

- Check ingredients on labels before using processed or prepared food. These often contain high levels of hidden sugar and fat.

- Slowly replace red meat (which tends to be high in fat) with low-fat, protein-rich foods such as chicken, fish or vegetarian substitutes like tofu or soya protein.

- Grill, steam or stir-fry food in preference to either shallow or deep frying it.

- If at all possible, use low-fat vegetable margarine rather than butter.

- If a sweetener is needed, consider adding fruit, such as bananas, dried fruit or even a little honey.

- Use skimmed or unsweetened soya milk rather than full-fat milk for cereals, tea, coffee, etc.

- Use low-fat cheese instead of a full-fat type.

- Use wholegrain bread, rather than white bread, as it is richer in minerals and vitamins, and has high levels of fibre, which makes it more filling.

- Scrub potatoes thoroughly, and cook them in their skins. Potatoes are a good source of vitamins, carbohydrates and fibre, and are only significantly fattening when fried or cooked in butter, etc.

- Consider replacing 'stodgy' traditional puddings with fresh fruit or low-fat yogurt.

- Switch from high-sugar fizzy drinks to low-calorie options or, better still, water or unsweetened fruit juices.

- Try to avoid snacks between meals.

- Do not buy biscuits, cakes or crisps – if they are *there* they will be eaten!

- Remember that alcoholic drinks contain very high levels of calories. This, again, is an increasingly important issue for people with mild learning disability who live independently.

Specific nutrients and dietary content
Protein

Approximately one fifth of an adult's body weight is made up of protein. Proteins are composed of several amino acids, and form the basic structural properties of cells. They are present in all the structural elements of the body, including muscle and skeleton, as well as in the enzymes that carry out chemical reactions in the body – such as those in the digestive system, which convert food into useful compounds. Various types of proteins are required, and all are made by the body itself from basic building blocks. Proteins are essential for the maintenance and repair of cells, for growth, for building new tissues and for the production of 22 specific amino acids, without which health cannot be maintained. A regular intake of protein is therefore required, particularly as it cannot be stored like fat. Excessive quantities, however, can reduce the absorption of minerals and vitamins, and protein is excreted if not required at a particular time.

Protein is present in most food groups, in different forms and quantities. Some high-protein foods, such as red meat, eggs and cheese, also contain high levels of fat, while others, such as beans and peas, contain little or none. Lean cuts of red meat are best, and excessive visible fat should be trimmed. Ideally, meat should be grilled, and fat allowed to drip away. Fish and chicken are valuable sources of protein, and generally contain less fat than red meat. Nuts are high in protein, and are recommended for people who want to follow a vegetarian diet. However, they are also high in fat.

Fats

Fats are one of the three main constituents of all foods and, although people are increasingly concerned about eating fat, it is, in fact, also important for a wide range of body functions. Fats can be stored in the body until required.

Fats and oils also contain essential vitamins, especially vitamins A and D, essential for calcium absorption (needed for strong bones and teeth). Vitamins A, D, E and K are the 'fat-soluble vitamins'. Unlike water-soluble vitamins, an excess of fat-soluble vitamins can be as harmful as a deficiency, so care needs to be taken if supplementation is given. Polyunsaturated fats are a special type of fat found in foods such as sunflower oil, olive oil and oily fish. They provide essential fatty acids, which are required in a wide range of body functions, especially in the nervous system. They differ in their chemical make up from saturated fats, which occur in foods such as butter, cream, lard and coconut oil. This latter type of fat is associated with health risks.

Although excessive fat and oil intake can cause a build-up of cholesterol, and also lead to weight problems (with the associated health risks), a totally fat-free diet is not appropriate, because some fat is essential for health and body maintenance. Cholesterol itself, though harmful in excess, plays an important role in the production of cell membranes, and assists the digestion of carbohydrates and the absorption of vitamin D. Over-consumption of food that is high in saturated fat, however, leads to excessive cholesterol build-up in arterial walls. When calcium is deposited along with the cholesterol (a process known as 'calcification'), this is known as 'atheroma', 'arteriosclerosis' or 'hardening of the arteries'. This not only increases the risk of a heart attack (due to narrowing of the internal diameter of the arteries) but also causes raised blood pressure, due to loss of arterial flexibility. This puts a strain on the heart and vascular system, and increases the risk of stroke. Healthy eating and exercise under medical supervision can assist in lowering seriously high cholesterol levels, which can be detected by a simple fasting blood test.

Carbohydrates

Valuable sources of energy-giving carbohydrates include pasta, bread (preferably wholemeal), potatoes, rice and other grains. Such foods have traditionally been considered (unfairly) as 'stodgy', and therefore fattening. Often, it is the oil, butter, cheese and other ingredients that are combined with these foods that are responsible for the higher fat contents.

Carbohydrates provide energy for all cells in the body. They contain carbon, hydrogen and oxygen, and are broken down into glucose in the body. This is carried around in the bloodstream to its final destination, which includes the muscles and the brain. Surplus glucose is stored in the liver and in muscles in the form of glycogen, until required by the body, when it is re-converted to glucose. There is a limit to how much glycogen can be stored in the liver, and any excess is therefore converted into fat.

Carbohydrates are the primary fuel-source for muscle contraction, and can provide energy to the muscles up to three times as fast as fat. In starvation, protein is also broken down into glucose, by a process known as 'gluconeogenesis'. This can lead to severe muscle and body wasting.

Vitamins and minerals

Vitamins are organic substances present in small amounts in most foods, and are essential, in varying quantities, for the healthy functioning of cells. A sensible and varied diet, including lots of fresh fruit and vegetables, ensures a sufficient intake of most vitamins, particularly if eaten raw.

Cooking causes some loss of vitamins, thus reducing the nutritional value of most fresh fruit and vegetables, so it is a good idea to eat several pieces of fruit and some raw vegetables daily. In fact vegetables that are rapidly frozen preserve their vitamin content better than some fresh vegetables left on the shelf for many days.

Leafy green vegetables are high in vitamin C, folic acid and vitamins E and K. They also contain a variety of minerals, including iron. Yellow and orange vegetables, such as carrots and most fruit, also contain high levels of vitamin A, in the form of carotene.

When preparing vegetables for cooking, preparation should be done at the last possible minute, in order to expose cut surfaces to the air as briefly as possible. Soaking of peeled or cut vegetables in water draws out valuable minerals and vitamins into the water, which is usually then discarded. Vegetables should be washed, scrubbed or scraped, and peeling should be avoided if possible, as many of the nutrients are just below the vegetable-skin surface. Vegetables should be briefly cooked in a pan with a tight lid, or steamed, rather than being cooked until soft and soggy.

Minerals are inorganic substances found in food from both animal and vegetable sources. Being inorganic means they are often chemically more stable than vitamins and not as affected by cooking etc. They are substances from the earth, and include iodine, boron, manganese, magnesium, copper, cyanide, arsenic, etc. The human body only requires these minerals in minute quantities, and, in the Western world, deficits are rare.

WHAT DO VITAMINS DO?	
Vitamin A	Important for eyesight and growth.
Vitamin B	Important for healthy nervous system and muscle activity.
Vitamin B2	Important for growth and the breakdown of protein and fats.
Vitamin B6	Healthy skin and nerve condition.
Vitamin B12	Making healthy blood cells and the formation of nerves.
Vitamin C	Immune system. Healing. Cell growth.
Vitamin D	Strong bones and teeth.
Vitamin E	Fights chemicals which can damage cells.
Folic Acid	Production of red blood cells.

CALCIUM

Calcium is a mineral that is essential for bones and teeth, as well as being needed in blood-clotting and nervous system function.

The body needs adequate vitamin D in the diet to allow calcium absorption. Dairy products are a good source of calcium, but are high in fat, so low-fat milk, cheese, etc. are preferable to full-fat types. Dark-green vegetables, wholegrain bread and fish (particularly fish with edible bones) are also important sources of calcium. Dietary deficiency in calcium results in weak bones and teeth and, in women (particularly after the menopause), to more severe osteoporosis, leading to increased risk of fractures.

IRON

Iron is mainly needed in the body to manufacture haemoglobin, which allows red blood cells to carry oxygen around the body. Iron is stored in the liver and bone marrow, and the average person has sufficient stores to last several months. Foods rich in iron include red meats and offal, such as liver. Iron is also present in egg yolks, raisins, chocolate and dried apricots. Iron requires vitamin C in order to be efficiently absorbed and so squeezing lemon juice onto meat and fish, which is a common practice in the Mediterranean, is a good idea. Iron deficiency causes anaemia, which may present with symptoms of fatigue or heart palpitations.

Women are much more at risk of iron deficiency than men, due to iron loss during periods or in pregnancy. In the Western world, iron-deficiency anaemia in non-vegetarian men is rare. Consequently, if this *is* found in a man, there should be further investigations to find the cause, as it may relate to chronic bleeding somewhere in the body (e.g. from a duodenal ulcer).

Fibre

This is a word used to describe substances mainly found in fruit and vegetables that make up the structure of the plant, mainly in the form of cellulose. This is not absorbed or digested, but nevertheless assists digestion by adding bulk to our food – thus enabling it to pass smoothly through the digestive system. A diet that is lacking in fibre leads to constipation, and in some people more serious diseases of the digestive system, like diverticulosis, or even cancer.

The best sources of dietary fibre are wholegrain cereals (particularly bran), vegetables, fruits and nuts. Unpolished brown rice, beans and pasta also contain high levels of fibre. Processed foods like white bread, white rice and white pasta have significantly lower fibre content than brown alternatives, and should ideally be avoided. Fibre provides satisfying bulk to meals, without adding sugar or calories. A simple way to increase fibre in the diet is to increase intake of fruit and vegetables, complete with their fibre-rich skins. However, it is important that fruit and vegetables are carefully washed to eliminate traces of pesticides. Ideally, organically grown crops may be best in this respect.

Sugar

It has long been known that refined sugar is bad for the teeth and causes weight gain. However, simple 'natural' sugars in the form of glucose and fructose ('fruit sugar'), found in sweets and dried fruit, provide immediately available energy, because they absorb directly into the blood without need of digestive activity.

It is important to remember that sugar only provides energy, and has no other food value. It should therefore not be consumed in excess of requirement. Sugar provides no vitamins or minerals needed by the body, and the body does not need sugar in the diet, as it can make its own sugar from other sources.

Studies suggest that people who eat large amounts of refined sugar in their diets have a higher incidence of coronary heart disease, obesity and diabetes. They also suffer a higher than usual incidence of tooth-decay.

Sugar is easy to remove from the diet, by substituting it with artificial sweeteners, or drinking 'diet' cold drinks, etc. It should be remembered that most carbonated drinks and pre-prepared meals are prone to having high sugar contents, so labels should be carefully read before buying.

Salt

Salt is essential in the human diet, is required for maintaining the correct blood pressure and is needed for nerve and muscle activity. Salt is lost from the body through perspiration, urine and faeces, and severe loss of salt will result in a dramatic, possibly fatal, drop in blood pressure. Salt is, however, present in most foods, and, except in extreme weather conditions, an adequate amount is readily available.

The unfortunate tendency of processed-food manufacturers to add excessive salt to their products, or of cooks to do the same at home, has resulted in unhealthily high levels of salt being consumed by many people. High blood pressure and heart disease can result from this, so a reduction in salt intake can help avoid those risks.

Exercise and people with learning disability

Encouraging people with learning disability to exercise can be a tricky subject. Many people with learning disability live sedentary lifestyles, with little planned, or even unplanned, exercise. What is provided for them in terms of exercise is often inappropriate or insufficient, e.g. a short trip to a gym, or a single swimming session per week. Often, carers looking after people with learning disability question why they remain obese in spite of partaking of such exercise, not realising that a half-hour swim burns fewer calories than two chocolate digestive biscuits, or that an hour on a weights machine is of little benefit to someone with a Body Mass Index (BMI) of 35.

When considering the benefits of exercise the basic principle to remember is that energy taken into the body should be equal to energy consumed, and that even minimal calorie intake above body requirement, over time, will lead to slow, but significant, weight gain. Exercise, in itself, unless on a daily basis for many hours and unless combined with dietary restriction, is unlikely to lead to significant weight loss in someone who is over-weight. For your information we provide in Table 3.3 a list of exercises with associated calorific use per hour.

Table 3.3 Calorie use per hour of aerobic exercise

Exercise	Calories used per hour
Cycling	300
Football	550
Jogging	600
Walking	250
Running	950
Swimming	500

Type of exercise

Exercise is generally divided into two types: anaerobic (in which muscles are not using oxygen at the time) and aerobic (using oxygen at the time).

- Anaerobic exercise (e.g. lifting heavy weights), which is associated with low oxygen levels in the tissues, is primarily an activity designed to increase muscle bulk and is not usually associated with significant weight loss. (Because oxygen is not consumed at the time by the muscles doing the work, an 'oxygen debt' is built up. In effect, the 'anaerobic' respiration leads to a build-up of lactic acid. Oxygen is needed in the metabolic process that breaks this acid down when the exercise is ended.)

- Aerobic exercises are types of exercise associated with burning calories and increasing cardiovascular reserve. This type of exercise is recognised as having significant health benefits. Examples include walking, running, swimming, cycling, etc. However, any type of activity that raises the pulse and respiratory rate above normal should be viewed as exercise. Table 3.4 shows some everyday activities, and the amount of calories they burn. As can be seen, even things such as housework or gardening are exercise, and should be encouraged.

Table 3.4 Calorie use per hour in daily activities

Activity	Calories used per hour
Sleeping	70
Ironing	250
Gardening	300
Watching TV	75
Making beds	150
Hoovering	180

Dangers of exercise

It is sometimes thought that for people with certain medical conditions exercise can be dangerous, if not fatal, and this view is often reinforced by the statement 'Seek medical advice before embarking on an exercise programme', which some companies include on their literature for fitness equipment or services. It is certainly true that caution does need to be exercised in the cases of people with heart disease (particularly with known ischemic problems, i.e. poor blood supply to the heart muscle, or structural heart problems like leaking or narrowed valves) or people with severe respiratory problems, and several endocrine disorders. Indeed, if the person for whom you care has any of the conditions listed below, we recommend you seek medical advice before embarking on an exercise programme:

- congestive cardiac failure.
- unstable angina
- abdominal aortic aneurysm
- congested heart disease (aortic stenosis)
- fever and infection
- deep-vein thrombosis

- detached retina or eye injury
- hernias.

However, this said, for most people with learning disability, a mild to moderate exercise regime can only be beneficial – particularly if started gently.

Chapter 4

Learning Disabilities and Mental Health

Perhaps surprisingly, people with learning disabilities have a much greater incidence of mental health problems (i.e. psychiatric illnesses that are different to the problems of learning disability itself) than the general population. Some studies suggest that 20 to 30 per cent of people with LD have some form of psychiatric or psychological difficulty, in addition to their learning disability.

However, in people with more severe disability, particularly where there are communication difficulties, it is frequently difficult for psychiatric illness to be diagnosed and treated. In this client group, some psychiatric conditions present as behavioural problems, such as aggression or self-injurious behaviour. Even in people with better communication skills, the presentation of psychiatric disorders is modified by the presence of the learning disability. Specialist assessment by a psychiatrist with expertise in mental illness in people with LD is therefore vital.

It is not uncommon for people with LD to have had their psychiatric illnesses for much longer periods than others in the general population, before a diagnosis is made and treatment offered. This can lead to secondary problems, for example severe self-injurious behaviour (e.g. damage to eyes, resulting in visual impairment or loss of sight; head-banging, leading to brain damage and epilepsy, etc.). This is particularly unfortunate where the cause is a treatable illness, such as depression, which has not been treated because the symptoms are thought to result from the learning disability. It is therefore important that such secondary problems are not allowed to occur.

There is always the danger in people with LD that any new symptoms or behaviour are thought to arise out of the learning disability when they do not. This phenomenon is called 'diagnostic overshadowing', and although primarily relating to symptoms of mental illness, it can also affect the diagnostic process for physical illnesses. Below is a list of factors that account for why people with LD have such high levels of psychiatric illness, compared with the general population.

Biological factors:

- *underlying brain damage* (e.g. cerebral palsy, rubella in pregnancy, birth anoxia)

- *genetic factors* e.g. Down's syndrome can be associated with dementia; tuberous sclerosis can be associated with autism; Prader-Willi syndrome can be associated with overeating and obesity, psychosis; Lesch-Nyhan syndrome can be associated with self-injurious behaviour

- *epilepsy* can lead to increased levels of psychiatric disorders, including depression and psychosis

- *sensory impairment* leads to a four-fold increase in psychiatric disorders

- *prescribed medication* leads to increased levels of psychiatric disorders precipitated by certain types of medication.

Psychological factors:

- poor communication skills
- limited range of coping behaviours
- low self-esteem, based on
- self-perceived history of 'failure'.

Social factors:

- *labelling* – the unhelpful and often derogatory terms attached to some people by wider society
- *loss* – e.g. bereavement/other substantial changes such as leaving parents to live in residence
- *sexuality* – e.g. inability to deal with it appropriately
- *limited relationships*
- *lack of achievement*, poor self-esteem.

Common psychiatric conditions associated with people with learning disabilities
Dementia

Dementia is usually a condition that occurs in older people. It is generally characterised by a 'global' (overall) loss of skills and abilities, which usually comes on over a number of years. It can be caused by a wide range of medical problems, including various infections affecting the brain, vitamin deficiencies or glandular problems (e.g. the thyroid), but more commonly it is due to either vascular problems (where the blood supply to the brain is interrupted by narrowing of arteries or small strokes), or Alzheimer's disease.

As the life expectancy for people with LD increases due to advances in neonatal, and other, medicine, it is becoming more common for these people to develop dementia. However, it is often a difficult diagnosis to make, particularly in the early stages, as the initial symptoms are often vague, and include subtle changes in personality, and such features as apathy, aggression, irritability and withdrawal. These symptoms can often be attributed to other causes, particularly if there are specific life events occurring at that time.

Problems also arise in spotting changes due to dementia in people with quite severe degrees of learning disabilities, when their initial level of adaptive functioning was already quite impaired. For example, in the general population someone with a moderate to severe degree of dementia may have problems dressing, washing themselves or communicating clearly. Someone with a severe learning disability may have never had these abilities in the first place.

Until recently there has been little in the way of active treatment for this type of condition, other than for the rarer types with 'reversible' causes, such as vitamin deficiencies, 'reversible' normal-pressure hydrocephaly, etc.

However, in recent years a number of drug treatments (anticholinesterase inhibitors) have become available, particularly used in cases of Alzheimer's disease. There is debate about their role in dementia, particularly for people with LD, but they seem to be beneficial, at least for some. It is important to make the diagnosis of dementia early, as the treatment appears to be more effective at that stage.

People with Down's syndrome are particularly prone to this dementia, and further discussion about this can be found in Chapter 5.

Drug- and alcohol-related mental health problems

Drug and alcohol problems are becoming increasingly common, particularly in people with mild degrees of learning disability who live alone. Although some are physically dependent on alcohol (i.e. suffer withdrawal symptoms, such as tremors and hallucinations, when they stop), the majority appear only to be psychologically dependent. There are two recognised reasons why people with LD drink alcohol excessively. There is a group of young men who see drinking as an important part of their social role as a man, and consequently spend much of their time in places where they are bought drinks by others. In situations like this, finding an alternative social role can help reduce alcohol abuse.

Another group are 'self medicating', to help with underlying psychiatric or psychological difficulties, particularly anxiety and depression. Sometimes this is seen in people living alone and struggling to cope. Under these circumstances, people often drink more regularly, and physical dependence can become a problem, eventually resulting in damage to other bodily systems, including the liver and central nervous system.

Affective disorders

Primarily a disorder of mood, these can present with depression (low mood), mania/hypomania (high mood) or a mixture of the two (Bipolar Affective disorder).

DEPRESSION

Depression is a very common psychiatric condition in people with LD, occurring in up to 10 per cent. In those with mild learning disability, it is usually straightforward to diagnose and treat because common symptoms, including feeling unhappy and tearful, are self-reported, so other people usually recognise there is a problem. However, in people with more severe degrees of disability, the symptoms are not self-reported, and 'classic' symptoms may not be so obvious.

Low mood might present in many ways, including irritability, self-injurious behaviour or even physical aggression. It must also be borne in mind that depression, like many other health problems, varies considerably in its severity from person to person. In some people it can be just mild feelings of unhappiness and dissatisfaction with life, often triggered by fairly clear understandable external events.

In other people, particularly where there is a family history of the condition, there may be a very serious mental health problem, associated with marked reduction in dietary and fluid intake. There may be no clear trigger for such illness episodes. It must always be remembered that before effective treatments were available for depression it was sometimes a fatal condition.

Fortunately there is now available a wide range of both psychological (talking therapies) and medical treatments – antidepressant medication and electroconvulsive therapy treatment (ECT) – so it is now fairly straightforward to treat depression once the diagnosis has been made. Depending on the cause of the condition, a combination of both medical and psychological interventions appears to work best.

MANIA/HYPOMANIA

This is less common than depression, and tends to come on more rapidly, and be of shorter duration. It commonly presents in adolescence, particularly in those with autism. It is characterised by problems in sleeping, overactivity, high and grandiose mood (e.g. thinking they are special/important, making grandiose plans involving others), irritability and aggression, talking fast, giggliness, disinhibition (doing things they would not usually do – e.g. having sex with strangers, masturbating in public/undressing/over familiarity/buying gifts for strangers, spending money to excess).

These problems can lead to serious problems if not managed quickly. When mania is severe, people can also have psychotic symptoms (see pages 54–55). Hypomania has all the symptoms of mania, but not delusions. If delusions are present (i.e. fixed, clearly false, ideas that are held against all evidence to the contrary), the condition is mania.

Medication that can help includes antipsychotics and mood stabilisers, and good support such as the following can also play an important role:

- observation to prevent harmful acts, avoid conflicts/ confrontation that can lead to aggression

- making the environment as safe as possible (e.g. by reducing access to potentially harmful things/situations)

- reducing stimulation (including caffeinated drinks, recreational drugs, loud music, etc.)

- encouraging exercise (more guidance on exercise is given on pages 44–46).

BIPOLAR AFFECTIVE DISORDER

Often people who have manic episodes also have periods of low mood. Sometimes there can be mixed symptoms of mania and depression within the same episode. If a person has either one or more manic episodes, or episodes of depression and of mania, this is classed as Bipolar Affective disorder. There may be long periods of stability between episodes, but episodes may become more frequent with increasing age.

Treatment includes managing acute episodes of depression or mania/hypomania, as described above. In addition, prophylactic treatment with mood stabilisers may help to reduce mood swings, and the onset of acute episodes.

Psychosis (including schizophrenia)

This group of disorders are disturbances of a person's experiences, affecting their thoughts, feelings and sensory perceptions. Such disorders can occur as part of illnesses (depression, mania, dementia) but are most commonly associated with schizophrenia, which affects up to 3 per cent of people with LD.

The following symptoms are 'psychotic' experiences.

- *Hallucinations* – These can occur in any sensory modality (i.e. hearing, vision, touch, smell, taste). The first two are the most common in psychiatric illness, the others sometimes an indicator of physical-health problems (organic disorder). In schizophrenia people may often describe 'voices' talking about them, or to each other. Sometimes the voices ask or tell people to do things ('command hallucinations') or can be very negative or insulting (derogatory). They are experienced as real, not the person's own thoughts, and are heard in external space. They can be very frightening to experience. If people cannot communicate that this is happening to them, it may be reflected in their behaviour, e.g. talking/shouting, indicating to something not there, irrational acts (when commanded) or preoccupation, and inattention to others.

- *Delusions* – These are fixed, clearly false, beliefs, out of the context of a person's experience, and unshakeably held. They can range from the extremely bizarre, to 'paranoid' thoughts that people or agencies are conspiring to harm them. Sometimes people feel their thoughts are being interfered with or their body functions are changed/out of their control (passivity experiences). They may think someone or something is putting thoughts directly into their head ('thought insertion'), or that they can put thoughts into others' heads ('thought broadcast'). The feeling of your thoughts not being your own is known as 'alienation of thought'. All of these experiences can be very distressing and lead to unusual behaviours, or sometimes risky acts (e.g. protecting oneself with violence /deliberate self-harm).

- *Thought disorder* – This happens when thoughts get confused, and speech gets mixed up. People may complain of very rapid, muddled thoughts. Speech may be very fast ('pressure of speech'), and not grammatically correct. There may be little or no logical linking between the topics discussed ('loosening of association'). Words or phrases may be in the wrong place. Ideas may jump from place to place, with no seeming pattern ('flights of ideas', 'knight's-move thinking'). 'Desultory thinking' may occur, which is shown as normal-sounding phrases or sentences being inappropriately juxtaposed with other phrases or sentences, without any logical connection. The train of thought may be so disturbed that words are placed so randomly and without logic as to render the speech completely incomprehensible ('word-salad' or 'schizophasia'). Sometimes new words/phrases (neologisms) may be made up. On the other hand, if the thoughts are slowed up and have little content, the speech may be very slow, with long pauses. 'Poverty of thought' may be present. There may be 'thought-blocking', in which the patient has the experience of their thoughts being 'blocked' or withdrawn from their head. Some people may even become mute.

Anxiety disorders

Our bodies and minds are programmed to react to stress, to best prepare us for either 'fight or flight'. Physical responses include heart-rate increase and faster breathing (both to increase oxygen levels), sweating (to cool us down), a dry mouth, muscular tension and aches, butterflies in the stomach, increased alertness and heightened senses. At a biological level, stress hormones, and adrenalin and noradrenalin, are released in high quantities, and blood is diverted to the muscles of locomotion, the heart and lungs, the brain and the sensory organs, particularly those involved in avoiding danger. Thus we are 'enabled' to either flee or fight for survival.

Mostly, we are able to utilise these responses to help us perform better in difficult or stressful situations (e.g. sitting an exam, speaking in public). However, if they become too out of proportion with the stress, they become a mental health problem.

There are a number of different types of anxiety disorder, as listed below, but all have the above symptoms at their core.

- *Generalised anxiety disorder* – This happens in many different contexts and can be long-standing and pervasive.

- *Phobia* – These are specific fears, about certain situations or things (e.g. heights, animals, etc.). These thoughts and fears are irrational/out of proportion and can include a fear of embarrassment or physical harm (e.g. having a heart attack). People will often avoid or run away from situations, which, in turn, reinforces the phobia.

- *Obsessive compulsive disorder* – These have two components:

  - Obsessive thoughts/images/impulses that are seen as the person's own, but are unwanted and often distressing. They may seem irrational or out of the control of the person experiencing them.

  - Compulsive acts/rituals are things that people do to help reduce the anxiety generated by compulsive thoughts, e.g. washing hands through fear of contamination. There may sometimes be a seemingly 'magical protective' quality to these routines, e.g. counting in certain ways, turning on/off light switches. People with autistic spectrum disorder may exhibit obsessive/compulsive features as part of the condition.

As can be seen above, anxiety disorders cover a wide range of conditions, all of which are characterised by the experience of worry or tension. This can occur at all times, and is then usually called a 'generalised anxiety disorder'. People complain of feeling afraid or 'on edge', or they have physical symptoms of anxiety, such as a racing heart-beat, tightness in the chest or 'butterflies' in the stomach. They may also feel nauseous, and may feel a need to 'escape'. Generalised anxiety by itself is a common condition, but can also be associated with other, more serious, psychiatric disorders, such as depression.

Sometimes anxiety occurs in particular situations, as discrete episodes of panic. An example is becoming particularly nervous or frightened in a crowded shop or public place, and feeling a need to flee the situation. Escaping that environment leads to a reduction of symptoms, which then reinforces future avoidant behaviour.

In people with LD, anxiety may be associated with anger or aggression, particularly if the person is forced to remain within the anxiety-provoking situation. An example is someone with autism having to attend a party and socialise. Feelings of anxiety can also be triggered by other specific situations or objects. This type of problem is called a 'phobia'. People with LD often have phobias about such things as spiders or other insects ('specific phobia'), and they are frequently also fearful of social situations ('social phobia').

Obsessive compulsive disorder (OCD) is another anxiety-related condition, in which people feel they have to carry out repetitive activities, despite recognising this as pointless, and not really wanting to do it. However, if they do not carry out the acts, they experience increasing anxiety and tension. In the end the only way out of their predicament is to give in to the obsession and perform the ritual or act. The rituals can be quite bizarre and unusual, but frequently involve cleanliness in some form (e.g. obsessive hand-washing).

For all anxiety disorders it is very important to ensure the symptoms are not indicative of another psychiatric problem, particularly if the onset is recent. The majority of anxiety disorders tend to be long-standing conditions, which have been present for many years. Acute onset should always arouse suspicion as to causation.

Depression is the most common psychiatric condition causing anxiety symptoms, and, if such symptoms arise where they were not previously present, this disorder must be considered.

Sometimes symptoms of anxiety are related to physical illness, including various glandular disturbances (an overactive thyroid), or cardiac problems. These should also be checked for.

Medication can play a useful part in the short-term treatment of anxiety disorders, but on the whole the most effective treatments are the talking therapies.

Post traumatic stress disorder (PTSD)

Serious life events can sometimes lead to profound psychological effects, which have not gone away with time (e.g. as the majority do). People can experience 'flashbacks', triggered by events, worry/apprehension, insomnia (poor sleep) and nightmares, irritability, and poor concentration. This can lead to loss of skills, drug/alcohol misuse and self-harm. People with LD may experience PTSD after seemingly less-traumatic experiences. They are also more prone to being the victims of abuse than other people are, which is clearly an upsetting experience.

Adjustment disorders

Adjustment disorders are conditions where an event in someone's life triggers a disturbance in their emotional well-being, or a change in their behaviour. They are strongly associated with anxiety disorders, but are a distinct entity. An example would be bereavement, or other major life event. People with LD are particularly susceptible to adjustment disorder, given their life-long dependence on others, and lack of autonomy. An example may be someone with a moderate degree of learning disability living with an elderly parent, who dies unexpectedly. This would be a great loss for anyone but is clearly especially difficult for someone who was very dependent on that parent.

People with LD, following the death of a parent, may be moved into residential accommodation, on an emergency basis, at short notice. This may be geographically remote from where they lived previously, so consequently they may stop attending accustomed day activities of many years. This may lead to the severance of close, cherished relationships, as well as a dramatic change of living style. There are many examples of large change in the lives of people with LD after bereavement.

Given the reduced range of social contacts that people with LD tend to have, changes in matters such as day-care settings can have major impacts. A key worker leaving to go on maternity leave or to take up another job is an example. The significance of a trusted mentor and friend should never be underestimated. In general, adjustment reactions are often associated with feelings of depression and anxiety, but in people with LD they may sometimes also be associated with disorders of conduct (e.g. behavioural problems like physical aggression or running away). On the whole, the treatment for such disorders is psychological in nature, although in some people short-term medication may be required in the early stages.

Supporting a person with their anxiety problems can be exhausting, but is also rewarding. A person may need medication if the problem is severe, but psychological and environmental support such as the following can play a big part:

- helping people to use relaxation techniques
- supporting people in stressful situations to challenge phobias in a gradual way ('graded exposure')
- reducing anxiety-provoking substances, e.g.
  - caffeine drinks
  - alcohol
  - cigarettes.
- gentle challenging of exaggerated beliefs
- encouraging people to 'ride out' panic attacks without fleeing the situation. Such attacks *do* pass, and usually nothing bad does happen. Riding out an attack helps re-programme the mind to 'give it a go' next time round.

Somatoform disorders

These disorders are conditions where emotional distress or upset is exhibited as symptoms of physical illness (from *soma* for the body). This can sometimes take the form of complaints of aches and pains in various parts of the body, a loss of function (e.g. weakness in an arm or leg, or problems with vision). Clearly, physical illness needs to be excluded before such a diagnosis can be made. Once the diagnosis is made, management necessarily involves recognising it as a psychiatric or psychological disturbance, rather than a physical illness. The best treatment for this disorder is one of the talking therapies, unless there is other significant psychiatric illness.

Anger-management problems

Problems with temper control and anger management are very common in people with LD, and are not usually categorised as psychiatric problems. However, in some people temper control can be so poor that it results in either damage to property, or assaults on others. Under these circumstances, a diagnosis of personality disorder is, unfortunately, sometimes made.

In people with LD, anger-management problems are sometimes considered as developmental in origin (i.e. temper tantrums are not uncommon in children, but are considered inappropriate in adults). Understanding anger-management problems can be difficult.

There may be underlying causes, such as depression – where irritability and loss of temper may occur. The majority of anger-management problems have a history going back to childhood, and poor anger management has become 'characteristic' in that person.

Formal anger-management courses can help. Affected people are taught practical techniques to control their temper and avoid future adverse consequences.

On occasion, medication can help, particularly low-dose neuroleptics, or medication usually used to treat epilepsy. This should be reserved for serious and ongoing cases.

Behavioural disorders

'Behaviour problems' or 'challenging behaviour' is often spoken of in connection with people with severe degrees of learning disabilities. However, this is a term that should be used with caution, particularly in clients with limited communication abilities. In practice, so-called behaviour problems can have a wide range of physical, psychiatric and psychological causes, and any analysis of a new type of 'behaviour problem' needs to take these potential causes into account. Below are some examples of health problems that can be causing behavioural difficulties:

- Physical pain can present as aggression or self-injurious behaviour.
  - Rheumatoid arthritis may present with people biting their joints (e.g. knuckles of the hand).
  - People may become aggressive with abdominal pain, such as that due to period pain or constipation.
  - Dental difficulties can sometimes present as refusal to eat or distress around meal-times.
- Heart problems, including heart failure secondary to heart-valve disease, can present as disturbed sleep patterns at night, precipitated by breathing difficulties.
- Epilepsy can present as irritability or aggression immediately prior to, during or after a seizure. Post-ictally various psychiatric conditions, such as depression or psychosis, can lead to self-injurious behaviour or aggression.
- A past history of physical or sexual abuse can lead to self-injurious behaviour or physical aggression.

Consequently, in anyone with a 'behavioural disorder', all these medical, psychiatric and psychological conditions need first to be considered and excluded. Clearly, in some people behavioural problems are just that, but even then there is invariably a cause. The function or 'utility' of the behaviour to the people with LD needs to be determined before anything can be done to address it.

Behavioural disorders may be a sign of dissatisfaction or unhappiness with a particular situation (e.g. somebody asked to do something they don't want to do, or, more commonly, an activity they enjoy is coming to an end). Behavioural disorders may be an attempt to communicate, particularly in someone with limited communication skills. Under such circumstances, improving or developing a useful communication system (e.g. using a Makaton, a form of sign language) can be of great help.

Behavioural disorders may be due to a lack of stimulation or structured activity. The assessment of behavioural disorders can be difficult and protracted, requiring the help of a wide range of professionals. In the UK, these professionals can be found in the local community learning disability teams.

If, after considering them, physical and/or psychiatric problems are excluded, a 'functional analysis' for what is causing the behaviour disorder is appropriate. The most basic of these is an ABC analysis (Antecedent–Behaviour–Consequence).

CARRYING OUT AN ABC ANALYSIS

The first point in the ABC analysis is to try and determine what antecedent, (i.e. things occurring before the behaviour) if any, may have triggered it. This might include changes of environment, curtailment of pleasurable activity, being asked to carry out a particular task (e.g. go to bed, wash up, etc.) or simply a change in routine in someone who finds change stressful. Examples may be something *not* happening that is expected, such as a day activity being cancelled, or a member of staff being unavailable due to being off sick.

The second part of the analysis looks at the behaviour of concern, and a clear description of the behaviour, and of the events occuring around the same time, is obtained.

The third part of the analysis looks at consequences of the behaviour. The purpose is to determine if the consequences may be reinforcing or encouraging the behaviour of concern. An example is a person not wanting to attend a day service, because of conflict with another client there. If in the morning they are physically aggressive and assault their carers, they may be told they cannot go to the day service, 'as punishment' (perhaps because it is unsafe to let them go). Either way, the consequences of the person's behaviour are that they achieve what they wanted.

An ABC analysis can give information about what may be causing the behaviour, and what can be done to rectify it. This may involve changing causes in the person's environment that trigger the behaviour, or stopping something that occurs *after* a behaviour, and reinforces it. Below are some common examples from clinical practice.

Common triggers:

- being asked to carry out a task
- noisy environments
- meal-times
- staff shifting change-over times
- times with reduced structured activity
- bedtimes
- engagement in personal hygiene tasks, e.g. teeth-cleaning, shaving
- transportation issues
- staffing changes
- breaks in regular routine, e.g. Bank Holidays.

Common rewards that reinforce a behaviour:

- withdrawal from an activity or situation
- quiet time
- one-to-one attention
- offers of food or drink or other forms of placation.

Identifying possible mental health problems

As stressed earlier, it is important to recognise mental health difficulties in people with LD at an early stage. The above provides some detail on the range of psychiatric conditions commonly associated with learning disability as an awareness of the nature of different conditions is useful. However, there are also other useful things to remember and tools that can be used.

Dr Steve Moss, a consultant research psychologist at the Estia Centre, a training research and development resource for those who support people with learning disabilities, based at Guy's Hospital, London, developed with colleagues a screening tool called the 'Psychiatric Assessment Schedules for Adults with Developmental Disabilities' or 'PAS-ADD' for short, which highlights certain behaviours and signs that may be indicative of mental health problems in the learning disabled (Moss *et al.* 1998). Copies of this can be obtained from the publishers, Pavilion, through the following web address: www.pasadd.co.uk/.

Below is a list of possible warning signs that further psychiatric or psychological evaluation may be required, through the GP.

Warning signs (new, or worsening of existing traits):

- a change in sleep pattern for no obvious reason. This might include too much sleep, problems getting to sleep, frequent waking through the night or waking very early in the morning, such as 4 to 5 am

- a loss of interest in or enjoyment of activities previously carried out

- a refusal or reluctance to go out into the community, or apparent fear, agitation or anxiety when out and about

- a reluctance to mix with other people

- a loss of established skills and abilities

- an increase or decrease (change) in levels of vocalisation

- appearing to be listening to something when there is nothing to listen to, or appearing distracted and looking around the room for no apparent reason

- the onset of self-injurious behaviour, for no apparent reason

- the onset of aggression or irritability.

Although this list is not exhaustive, if any of these behaviours are identified, further evaluation may be appropriate, particularly if a number of the changes occur at the same time.

What to do if you suspect a psychiatric disorder?

Most psychiatric illness in the UK is treated by general practitioners, and this should be the starting point. However, should the GP have difficulty deciding what the problem is, or how to treat it, then they will usually make a referral to a specialist learning-disability psychiatrist, now available in most areas of the UK. Specialist learning-disability psychiatrists work in hospitals and in the community. In the community, they work in two roles:

1. as specialist doctors in the psychiatry of learning disability, who run outpatient clinics for people with learning disabilities who have problems with their mental health, behaviour or other conditions such as epilepsy, and

2. as part of a multi-disciplinary team comprising psychiatrists, psychologists, learning-disability nurses, occupational and speech therapists and other professionals.

Given some of the difficulties previously outlined in making diagnoses, a number of visits may be required, and information may need to be collected from various sources and taken into account.

The types of treatments available are divided up into:

- medication (various 'psychotropic' drugs)

- talking treatments (various types of psychotherapy)

- psychosocial treatments. These include modifications to a person's living environment, in order to improve their well-being. An example would be providing day activities, or modification to a residential living environment.

In fact, at any time up to 30 per cent of people with LD are taking some form of psychotropic medication for one reason or another.

As someone caring for a person with learning disability, following the initial recognition of suspected mental illness, an important task for you is to monitor medication side-effects, as many psychotropic drugs unfortunately do tend to cause these. A list of psychotropic drugs, with some examples of commonly encountered side-effects, is given in Table 4.1.

Usually the doctor prescribing the treatment monitors the client quite regularly initially, to ensure the treatment is helping. However he may ask the carer to monitor certain things to help them with their decision-making. These may include keeping records of sleep pattern, dietary intake, weight, severity and frequency of various behaviours, and other factors, depending what the underlying psychiatric condition is.

Table 4.1 The side-effects of psychotropic drugs

Type of drug	Condition treated	Commonly used medications	Side-effects
Neuroleptics	'Psychosis'	Risperidone; Clopixol Olanzapine, Quetiapine, Haloperidol, Chlorpromazine	Sedation, weight gain, stiffness/ shaking, extrapyramidal 'symptoms', blurred vision. Some may need regular blood monitoring
Anti-depressants	Depression	SSRIs (Serotonin Selective Reuptake Inhibitors), e.g. Fluoxetine, Paroxetine, Citalopram; Tricyclics, e.g. Amitriptyline, Nortryptillene, Lofepramine; Monoamine Oxidase Inhibitors, e.g. Tranylcypramine; Others, e.g. Venlafaxine, Duloxetine, Mirtazapine	Depend on the class of medication, but can include: sedation, dry mouth, nervousness, nausea, blurred vision, headache. Some drugs cause problems on stopping ('discontinuation syndrome')
Mood stabilisers	Bipolar disorder, epilepsy	Anti-epileptics, e.g. Carbamazepine, Valproate (including Sodium Semi-Valproate or 'Depokote'), Lithium Carbonate/Citrate	Weight gain, sedation, hair loss, foetal abnormalities. Some (such as Lithium Carbonate/ Citrate) need close monitoring have severe toxic side-effects if doses too high

Chapter 5

Physical and Mental Health Needs of People with Down's Syndrome[1]

This chapter is dedicated specifically to the health needs of people with Down's syndrome, the underlying causes of which are covered in more detail in the Appendix at the end of this book on genetic causes of learning disability (p.144). We have dedicated a whole chapter specifically to Down's syndrome here as it is a common form of learning disability and one that is accompanied by a particular set of health problems. People with Down's syndrome have the same medical and mental health problems as anybody else, but there are particular problems they are more prone to. Other areas of this book cover some of these. The following pages focus on a few in more detail.

Physical-health issues
Hormonal systems and body metabolism
A number of body 'systems' can be affected by Down's syndrome. These include the following.

- *Obesity* is an increasing problem in this country in general, but it is a particular problem for people with learning disability and Down's syndrome. Research shows that only 12 per cent of people with Down's syndrome have a 'desirable weight', with up to 25 per cent having medically significant obesity (i.e. it will affect their health). Obesity brings with it increased risks of a number of problems, including diabetes, heart disease, difficulty breathing at night (sleep apnoea) and strain on joints. It is therefore essential that, from an early age, a healthy diet is encouraged, along with ensuring reasonable levels of activity and exercise as part of a regular routine.

- *Thyroid disorders.* The thyroid gland (in the neck) makes the hormone thyroxine, which helps regulate the body's metabolism. Most commonly, people with Down's syndrome have under-active thyroid glands (hypothyroidism). This may cause slowing down, weight gain, constipation, abdominal pain, tiredness and apparent loss of skills. It can also lead to heart problems. These features are often difficult to notice early, so hypothyroidism is often diagnosed quite late. However, it is relatively easy to treat by replacing thyroxine in tablet form. It is recommended that people with Down's syndrome have regular tests of their thyroid gland (at least 2–3 yearly), so that problems are detected early.

- *Diabetes mellitus* (high blood sugar). Most commonly, people with Down's syndrome develop diabetes as a result of being over-weight (type 2, 'maturity onset' diabetes). Symptoms include thirst, excessive urination, weight changes, skin infections and visual problems. Again, symptoms may be rather vague, so the condition is often diagnosed late. It is important to manage high blood sugar, as it can lead to long-term damage in many areas of the body. The diagnosis is confirmed by blood tests, and treatments include alterations to diet, exercise, oral hypoglycaemic drugs and, in some cases, injections of insulin.

- *Menstrual (period) problems* in women. Most young women with Down's syndrome start periods at the same age as those without LD (age 10–14), but there may be an earlier menopause (when periods dwindle and stop). Most have uneventful, regular periods, but significant numbers may have problems that can include: premenstrual syndrome (tension), emotional and physical changes in the two weeks before menstruation. Simple measures such as hot water bottles and sympathy can help. Mild pain killers, oral contraceptives and other treatments may be suggested by a GP if problems are severe. Over the counter remedies such as evening primrose oil and other alternative therapies may have some benefits, but care and medical advice needs to be taken as these can affect other medications and some health conditions e.g. epilepsy. Painful periods (Dysmenorrhoea); absence of periods (Amenorrhoea); irregular periods (Oligomenorrhoea) and heavy periods (Menorrhagia) can also cause distress and concern to the individual and their carers. It is important to seek medical advice about such problems, particularly if there is a change to menstrual cycles or if bleeding happens between periods ('spotting'). Most people will only require simple interventions like pain relief, but some may need further investigation to exclude more serious conditions.

Blood disorders

A number of blood disorders are associated with Down's syndrome. These include:

- *Anaemia* (low levels of oxygen-carrying haemoglobin in the blood). Symptoms include exhaustion, dizziness, fainting, breathlessness, fast heart rate (tachycardia) and pallor.

- *Aplastic anaemia* (reduced production of all blood cells from bone marrow). Symptoms are similar to anaemia, but there is also an increased risk of infection, bruising and bleeding.

- *Polycythaemia* (increased red blood cells). Symptoms include headaches, blurred vision, high blood pressure, tiredness, circulatory problems and gout.

- *Leukaemia* (cancer of the white blood cells). Symptoms include tiredness, fever, infections, swollen glands, swollen abdomen with enlarged liver and spleen, bruising and pallor.

All these disorders can be detected by simple blood tests, although some may need further confirmation by taking small samples of bone marrow (biopsies). Other specialist tests, such as CT/MRI scans, may also be needed. The treatment of these conditions varies from simple iron supplements and dietary changes, to bone marrow replacement, blood transfusions and specialist chemo/radiotherapy. The recommendation is that people with Down's syndrome have a blood screen every 2–3 years.

Sensory problems

- *Hearing impairment.* People with Down's syndrome frequently have hearing problems, and some degree of deafness will affect most subjects at some point in their lives. Particular difficulties arise because they often have narrow ear canals, which increases the risk of recurrent infections and excessive wax impaction. Mild to moderate hearing loss can often go unrecognised. Suspicion should be raised if a person is not responding to sound, has particular difficulties learning, becomes withdrawn and quiet or appears not to respond to communication. There can also be an increase in behavioural and emotional problems. Investigations include formal hearing assessment, and examination. This may need to be done in a specialist centre, or by the GP. More serious conditions may need specialist treatments. It is recommended that hearing is tested every 1–2 years in people with Down's syndrome.

- *Visual impairment.* A distinctive feature of Down's syndrome is the outward-looking appearance of the eyes. A number of other abnormalities may occur, including:

- Problems focusing (short sightedness–myopia; long sightedness – hypermetropia). Corrective glasses may be required.

- Occasionally the central part of the covering of the eye (cornea) can protrude. This is called 'keratoconus', and it may need treatment and occasionally even surgery.

- A common condition is inflammation of the eyelids (blepharitis), which may need regular cleaning, and antibiotics.

- Quite often cataracts will develop (clouding of the eye lens), and result in gradual loss of vision. Severe cases may need surgery.

Any visual impairment can be associated with changes in behaviour and loss of skills. It is recommended that vision is checked every 1–2 years in someone with Down's syndrome.

Musculo-skeletal problems

People with Down's syndrome may develop joint problems as a result of excessive weight. Also, they tend to have lax ligaments stabilising their joints, which can result in dislocations.

Instability can occur in the joints at the top of the spine and the base of the skull, known as Atlanto Occipital instability (AOI), or between the first two joints of the spine, Atlanto Axial instability (AAI). There are usually no symptoms or signs, but excessive movement can result in spinal nerve injury. This can cause weakness in the arms and legs, and local discomfort. The condition is diagnosed by X-ray or CT scan of the upper spine. If it is present, caution is required with over-extension of the neck (e.g. when having a general anaesthetic). Exclusion from vigorous sporting activities may also be advised. If the condition is causing symptoms, surgical intervention may be required.

Respiratory problems

People with Down's syndrome suffer from the normal range of respiratory problems. However, chest infections and breathing problems are more common than in the general population, and remain a major cause of death in adults with Down's syndrome. If breathing symptoms are severe or prolonged, a medical opinion should always be sought.

A particular condition in Down's, associated with obesity and having a broad, short neck, is obstructive sleep apnoea (OSA). This occurs when the breathing tube (trachea) is closed off by the soft tissues of the throat during sleep. This may result in the person ceasing to breathe for a short time, eventually waking in order to breathe again. This cycle may occur many times in the night. Symptoms include disturbed sleep, with loud snoring, nocturnal choking, daytime sleepiness, morning headache, general irritability and poor concentration.

Obstructive sleep apnoea (OSA) is confirmed by watching the person sleep at night (sometimes using video recording), while measuring bodily functions, such as muscle tone and blood oxygen saturation. Treatment includes a number of measures, such as weight loss and avoidance of sedating drugs. In severe cases, people may need to be given oxygen and air at night, through a special face mask. This is called 'continuous positive airway pressure treatment' (CPAP).

Heart and circulation (cardiovascular) disorders

Throughout life, people with Down's syndrome are subject to the same problems as the general population. However, there are some particular areas of concern.

People with Down's syndrome often have 'congenital' heart problems. There are a number of these malformations, including holes in the various walls separating different parts of the heart (septal defects), faulty valves (which regulate blood flow), and parts of the heart and important blood vessels being connected in the wrong way. Most of these conditions are picked up soon after birth. Some require surgical treatment, while others improve as the heart develops. It is important to remember that people with certain heart defects may require antibiotic cover when they have surgical procedures (e.g. dental extraction, operations, etc), as if bacteria are released into the blood during these proceedures they can cause infection of the heart valves.

Severe obesity (see pp.32–35) can result in increased risk of high blood pressure and ischemic heart disease (insufficient blood flow to the heart muscle). This can cause 'angina' or chest pain, and can lead to death of part of the heart muscle – an infarction or 'heart attack'. Some people may develop shortness of breath, and poor exercise tolerance, due to heart failure.

Blood pressure and pulse can be reviewed at well-person checks with a GP practice nurse. These are basic checks offered by many GPs and will look at issues such as high blood pressure, diabetes and obesity. Should a heart murmur or severe shortness of breath develop, a special scan of the heart (echocardiogram) may be needed in order to exclude developing valve problems.

Digestive system (gastrointestinal)

Eating problems are common in people with LD, as are general abdominal aches and pains. This includes people with Down's syndrome. A healthy diet, good fluid intake and regular exercise can reduce the incidence of constipation. Persistent abdominal pain and other symptoms may require further assessment.

Dental care is important for every person with LD. They may have lower standards of dental hygiene because of difficulties with brushing and may also have difficulties in communicating dental pain. In addition, some syndromes cause problems with enamel formation. The recommendation is that a person with Down's syndrome should visit their dentist at least every 1–2 years, and preferably more often.

Skin (dermatological), hair and nail conditions

Problems affecting the skin, hair and nails care are very common in people with learning disabilities. Although many such problems are not serious, they do cause long-standing distress and discomfort, and are often easily treatable once recognised. Apart from conditions such as eczema and psoriasis, as in the rest of the population, people with LD are prone to develop various infections or infestations.

The reasons are probably multi-factorial, but group living is a major contribution.

Scabies, a parasitic infection, is a particularly common problem. It is often misdiagnosed as eczema or psoriasis, particularly when long-standing, and when scratching has led to secondary bacterial infection. Scabies causes a great deal of distress, with severe itching of the hands and groin region, which is much worse at night. It usually starts in the web spaces of the hands, and can be seen as small tracks where the insects burrow under the skin.

After a few days of scratching to relieve the intense itching, secondary bacterial infections may cause the condition to be mistaken for something else. Scabies can affect any part of the body, including the trunk, and any person with what appears to be skin irritation, particularly if others have similar symptoms, should be suspected of suffering from scabies. It is a relatively easy condition to treat with topical skin preparations; however, care should be used in deciding which one to use, particularly if the subject suffers from epilepsy, as some preparations can worsen seizures. A GP or pharmacist can give further advice.

Fungal infections are also common. They often affect moist areas of the body, such as the groin and armpit regions, or under the breasts in women. Again, these are relatively easy to treat with topical preparations, although in some instances their presence suggests other medical problems, such as diabetes. It is always worth screening for diabetes if people appear prone to this type of infection. Fungal infections can also affect the scalp (leading to hair loss) and the nails (leading to unsightly, thickened, discoloured toenails).

Fungal nail infections are extremely common in people with LD, and often go untreated. Although they don't cause significant health problems, they are unsightly, and spread easily, particularly in places like shared bathrooms. Finger and toenail infections are notoriously difficult to treat, mainly because the nail itself is 'dead' and has no blood supply. On balance, the best treatment appears to be daily application of topical nail paints for long periods of time, so that the new nail can grow through uninfected. There are oral treatments available, but risks of serious side-effects limit their use.

Some skin conditions in people with learning disabilities are associated with the underlying cause of their disorder. Examples include tuberous sclerosis and von Recklinghausen's disease (neurofibromatosis).

There is a growing body of knowledge about the management of skin and nail disorders, and referral to dermatologists who have a special interest in these conditions is sometimes advisable.

Nervous (Neurological) system

All types of neurological problems can occur in people with LD, and this includes people with Down's syndrome. They have significantly higher rates of epilepsy, which is often present from childhood or early adulthood. It can present in a variety of ways.

Epilepsy can also develop in older people with Down's syndrome (see pp. 91–101). This may herald underlying structural changes to the brain. If associated with loss of skills over time, it may indicate a dementing process (Alzheimer's disease), described later. If there is concern about persistent symptoms, medical opinion should be sought.

Psychological and emotional problems

PERSONALITY AND BEHAVIOURAL TRAITS

People with Down's syndrome, like everyone else, have their own personalities and idiosyncrasies. However, some behavioural and personality traits seem to be shared. This is known as a 'behavioural phenotype'. The best-known traits are those of being happy, gentle and eager to please. However, some people with Down's syndrome may seem stubborn and resistant to change, preferring set routines and requiring a structured day. Indeed, some people with Down's may also be diagnosed as having an autistic spectrum disorder.

DEPRESSION

People with LD, and particularly those with Down's syndrome, are more likely to become depressed than members of the general population. Features include seeming sad, becoming more isolated and less interactive, losing skills, going off food and losing weight.

Some people may experience hearing voices and start to believe strange, illogical things (delusions). In others, their behaviour may deteriorate in a number of ways, e.g. becoming irritable, aggressive and destructive. Depression may respond to the talking therapies and antidepressant medication. It may be associated with loss events (e.g. bereavement, moving home, etc). In some, it may be secondary to medical problems (e.g. hypothyroidism), and in others (particularly the elderly) it may herald the onset of a dementing illness (about which there is more below).

DEMENTIA (ALZHEIMER'S DISEASE)

This is a progressive deterioration of brain structure and function, which affects the memory, thinking, understanding and learning. It may present as a change in social behaviours, skills and physical health – the earliest features may be a change in personality, depression, loss of memory, mild disorientation, apathy, inattention and loss of skills. With time, these problems may increase. Some people go on to develop physical problems (e.g. deteriorating mobility, epilepsy), strange beliefs or abnormal experiences, such as auditory hallucinations (e.g. hearing somebody speak when there is no one there). The diagnosis of dementia must be made by a specialist (Consultant Psychiatrist) working with people with LD and will involve a number of investigations (to exclude physical causes), as well as serial ability and skills assessments. Though the development of dementia can, in some cases, be slowed by the use of medication, the disease will gradually progress. Eventually the person's physical health will deteriorate to the point where they may succumb to an infection or other terminal event. It is important that carers are aware that the older a person with Down's is, the more prone they will be to dementia. Early detection of the features of Alzheimer's disease can be beneficial, allowing earlier intervention, such as medication. Also, carers are then better placed to seek advice and support about how best to manage future care needs. Often this will be complex, needing a wide variety of professionals (e.g. social workers, occupational therapists, nurses and psychologists). (For more on dementia, see page 49.)

Medical checklist

More than is the case with the general population, it is important for individuals with Down's syndrome to receive regular health reviews and have regular health care 'check-ups'. This applies to adults with Down's syndrome of all ages. In Box 5.1 there is a checklist suggested by Professor Vee Prasher and Beryl Smith (Prasher and Smith 2002). The checklist summarises basic health issues and suggest routine checks for professionals and carers, and lists possible interventions where appropriate.

A detailed medical history and physical and psychological examination are the basis of all good health assessment. If health problems occur in someone you are caring for, a medical opinion should always be considered.

Box 5.1 Important health issues requiring regular checks in people with Down's syndrome

Particular problems for carers to be aware of:

Obesity	Depression
Dental problems	Behavioural difficulties
Sleep apnoea	Loss of hearing
Menstrual problems	Seizures
Decline in vision	Dementia
Heart failure	Delayed sexual development

Particular areas of health for professionals to observe

Weight	Dementia
Epilepsy	Sexual awareness
Depression	Menstrual cycle
Ears (hearing)	Thyroid disease
Eyes (visual acuity, cataracts, keratoconos)	Behavioural difficulties
	Medication
Heart murmur	
Dental health	

Box 5.1 Important health issues requiring regular checks in people with Down's syndrome *cont.*

Routine checks carers and professionals should be aware of

Measure weight at least once a year

Vision every 1–2 years

Hearing every 1–2 years

Teeth every 1–2 years minimum

Thyroid function tests every 2–3 years

Breast examination

Echocardiogram if heart murmur develops (exclude mitral valve prolapse)

Psychological status every 1–2 years (particularly over 40)

Review of medication every year

Areas of further intervention by carers and professionals

Education regarding basic health issues

Advice regarding particular health issues, e.g. dental care, obesity, hypothyroidism

Epilepsy

Parent/carer support groups

Recreational/vocational programmes

Sex education

Consent issues (supporting clients regarding their capacity to make decisions

How to access health and social services

Available residential facilities

Bereavement counselling for those who experience loss

Notes

1   Much of the information contained in Chapter 5 and Box 5.1 was summarised from *Down Syndrome and Health Care* Prasher and Smith (2002) with kind permission from BILD publications. Other useful references and sources of information are Prasher and Janicki (2002).

Chapter 6

Learning Disability, Health and the Law

The guidance and laws pertaining to physical and mental health problems have some overlap, but there are some important differences. If you are caring for someone who has mental health problems, it is therefore very important to be aware of the law in relation to both of these health areas and how this affects you and the person you care for.

Learning disability, mental health and the law

Most countries have their own Mental Health Legislation. In England, Northern Ireland and Wales the Mental Health Act is a piece of legislation that came into being in 1957, was updated in 1983 and further updated in 2008 (enactment of MHA 2007).

This Act allows people who are suffering with mental disorders, who might not themselves recognise the need for treatment, to receive against their will (under compulsion). There are many sections to this Act, which allows people to be admitted to hospital against their will, for periods of assessment and/or treatment. Some people call this 'sectioning', though professionals would use the term 'detention'. The act also allows people to be diverted from the criminal justice system into the hospital system, should it be felt that a mental disorder has played a part in their offending behaviour, or they become mentally unwell whilst in prison.

In the general population the most common reasons for being detained in hospital for treatment are various forms of severe mental illness, and this can also be applicable in people with learning disability. However, people with learning disabilities can also be detained in hospital when there is no diagnosed severe mental illness.

This can only take place if they have a significant impairment of social functioning (i.e. they have problems with relationships and living unsupported without help) and also show either abnormally aggressive or seriously irresponsible conduct, of a nature and / or degree as to warrant treatment in hospital for their own or others safety, or to prevent worsening of their condition. Before the recent amendments to the MHA, these conditions were defined legally as 'mental impairment' and 'severe mental impairment' (relating to the degree of LD). The law is there to protect the rights of people with a learning disability and it must be emphasised that it is not legally acceptable to detain someone in hospital merely on the basis that they have a learning disability.

Learning disability, physical health and the law

Until recently, there was no specific statutory legislation giving guidance on the treatment of physical illness for those unable to give valid consent (those who lacked the necessary capacity to do so).

In 2007 the Mental Capacity Act (2005) (MCA) was implemented in England, Wales and Northern Ireland. Similar legislation has been enacted in many countries, so the English system is used here only as an example of what the authors believe to be good practice. These laws provide a statutory framework under which decisions can be made for people who lack capacity. The legislation should be taken into account as a starting point for all self-care decisions for any individual over the age of 16.

Prior to this Act there was a lot of confusion surrounding this often complicated area. Decisions about physical health care for the mentally incapacitated previously had to be made within the 'common law', supported on occasions by 'case law', put forward by solicitors. Individual cases were decided in court by Judges and decisions were based on 'Best Management Principles'. Since April 2007 the new MCA (2005) has propelled common law management of the incapacitated into Statute Law, with clearer guidance, rights and responsibilities spelt out.

Many carers and some health care professionals, worry that giving treatment without valid consent could be construed as assault and legal action taken against them. This is true only if the person being treated is 'competent' (has capacity). The MCA now offers greater legal protection, if followed appropriately, for carers and professionals supporting patients who are not competent (lack capacity). Over time it should dispel previous myths and confusion surrounding this area and improve access to health care for this vulnerable group.

Defining 'competence' (capacity)

Put most simply, capacity is a person's ability to understand something. As such it is relevant to everything a person with learning disability does or is asked to do. There are a number of elements that make up capacity. In relation to understanding health problems, these include:

- the ability to know what the health condition they are suffering from is
- what treatments are available
- what the likely outcomes of any treatment might be (both good and bad)
- what the likely outcome of not having any treatment might be
- the ability to remember this information
- the ability to make a judgement by weighing up the information
- the overall ability to communicate their understanding and decision.

If the person you are caring for is able to satisfy all the above elements, and in their own mind they decide that they do not want the treatment, then obviously that is their decision to make – this applies to any adult whether or not they have a learning disability. If the person is an adult and is competent (i.e. has capacity) physical health treatments can not then be forced on them.

If, as a carer you are trying to work out whether a person has capacity for something it is also important to remember that:

- Capacity can change over time. For example, a person with a urine infection may become acutely confused for a short period. At that time they may lack capacity to agree to antibiotic treatment. However, after a short while on these medications, the initial infection may settle, and they might regain capacity to agree with continuing the course; a person with Dementia may have more lucid days or time of day, when they are better able to make decisions about any treatments needed. Always try to pick the best time to talk things through.

- Capacity is specific only to the particular treatment or thing a person is asked to consider or do. The amount of information that needs to be given to a person, and understood, about a proposed treatment depends on the seriousness of the implications of either receiving or not receiving that treatment. Consider the taking of a blood sample. This is a relatively safe procedure that most people have experienced at some point. When a doctor suggests a blood test, most patients will roll up their sleeve and expose their arm for the needle. In doing so, they indicate their consent. The doctor will not usually explain to the patient all the potential severe complications that may result (e.g. the needle may possibly pierce a nerve and the puncture wound may become badly infected etc.), only the most common (e.g. it may hurt and there may be a little bruising). However, if the doctor suggests a controversial form of treatment which has a high risk of failure or severe side effects, then clearly more time should be spent providing the patient with sufficient information to enable an informed decision to be reached.

- A person's capacity will vary with the degree of learning disability they have. As such a person with a mild disability might be able to make competent decisions about more complex health issues compared to someone with severe disability.

- People are allowed to make, what seem to others to be, unwise decisions, as long as they have the capacity to make that decision. Examples from everyday life include Jehova's Witnesses refusing blood transfusions even if it means them dying, and people refusing cancer treatments that might prolong their life.

What is Consent and what happens when someone lacks capacity?

Put most simply, consent is when someone agrees with or allows something to be done. In relation to health matters consent may be 'active / valid' in that the person fully understands what is asked of them (i.e. has capacity) and clearly expresses in words, writing or other ways that they understand what is proposed and are happy to go along with what is suggested without resistance.

'Implied / Passive' consent is when a person does not offer a clear opinion about their understanding and preference or blatantly lacks capacity, but when asked to do something will go ahead with it without significant resistance or need for major intervention (e.g. restraint). This sort of consent may often be the case with people with severe or profound learning disability. This 'implied' consent may be acceptable in respect of minor procedures (see example of blood test above), however, when a more risky or invasive form of investigation or treatment is suggested consent should be formally obtained in writing.

There are some mistaken beliefs about who should sign the consent form for those lacking capacity. These include the idea that it should be a family member, paid carer or the person's care manager. In fact it is the professional carrying out the procedure who should sign on behalf of the person lacking capacity to consent. Some Health and Social Care professions may be reluctant to do this, believing that if a person with learning disability cannot sign a consent form for a particular procedure or operation, and they seem resistive, then that procedure or operation cannot legally be carried out. This is not the case and is one of the barriers that needs to be overcome to improve access to appropriate care.

An example of what should happen is as follows: A person with sever LD has major problems with dribbling, which has not responded to medicines and other non invasive measures. Surgery to the salivary glands is suggested by a surgeon, this will prevent dribbling and may significantly improve the quality of life and allow greater community access. This requires an anaesthetic and is a somewhat controversial treatment with potential other risks. However, it is a non urgent treatment and under these circumstances it would be best for a multi disciplinary meeting to be held, including carers, relatives, the patients GP and other relevant parties such as advocates (if no relatives) , the anaesthetist and the surgeon proposing and performing the treatment. The 'best interests' of the patient should be at the heart of this meeting and determine the outcome. When having such a 'Best Interest' meeting, consideration will need to be made as to the practicalities of supporting any intervention or treatment (e.g. the use of restraint if the person resists, the use of sedative medications, levels of staffing needed at the time and for monitoring and support afterwards etc). If the person with LD who lacks capacity does not have a family carer or external advocates / friends to offer a view on what might be in their 'best interest', an Independent Mental Capacity Advocate (IMCA) may need to be appointed. Once everyone has given their opinion (which should be documented) and everyone is happy with the decision to go ahead, then the surgeon will make all necessary arrangements with the support of the carers and sign consent forms on behalf of the patient.

If the intervention is an extremely controversial one (e.g. sterilisation, termination of a pregnancy), or if everyone cannot agree what is in the persons best interest, then a Best Interest Meeting in itself is not enough to go ahead with treatment. In these cases the Courts will need to be involved in the process of coming to a decision. If either the carers/relatives views, or that of the professional, are felt to be unreasonable then a judge will make the final decision whether something can legally go ahead. In England and Wales judges are also available 24 hours a day (via the Guardianship Office and Court of Protection) to be called on by professionals for rulings on emergency situations.

Figure 6.1. is an illustration showing a decision making process on management of consent to capacity issues for people with LD in different situations, and provides a useful summary. We have provided further information in Chapter 4 on the circumstances under which it is necessary to admit someone with a learning disability to psychiatric care.

What is the situation for Children?

The Mental Capacity Act applies to people over the age of 16, but its principles and process are still useful when thinking about capacity issues in older children. Children under the age of 16 can themselves consent to many treatments (e.g. taking pain killers, going on the oral contraceptive pill), if they have capacity and are deemed competent to do so. In such instances their consent is legally valid. However, should a child under 16 refuse a course of treatment to which the parents agree, then currently the parents' decision prevails. The legal position in such situations in the UK can be complex, but is principally governed by the Children's Act (1989 and 2004). However, the MCA, Family Law Reform Act 1969, Human Rights Act 1998 and the United Nations Convention on the Rights of the Child and their relevant codes of practices all need to be considered. Because statutory law cannot cover all possible situations, decision making may continually be affected by changes to case law. This is when the circumstances of individual cases are considered, and decisions made, by the Courts, usually guided by precedent.

In general, where ever possible, for children under the age of 16 requiring treatment parental consent should always be sought. This may not be possible in extreme emergencies. If parental consent appears to be unreasonably withheld, and there is a risk of serious harm to the child, it may be necessary to consider legally replacing the parents as guardians through the Courts, with the involvement of Social Services.

It is also important to know that if a child has a mental disorder, the Mental Health Act can also be applied, for the same reasons as it is used for in adults (see earlier). It has no minimum age limit.

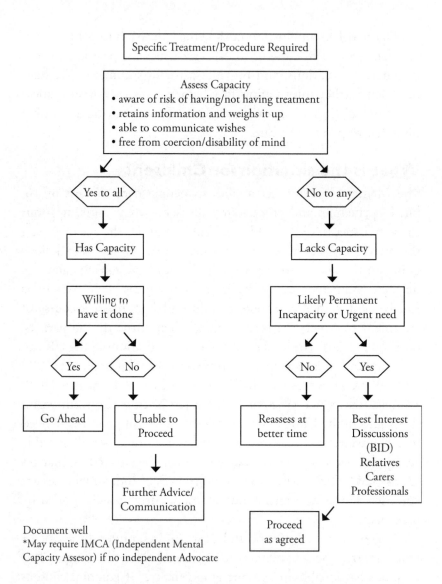

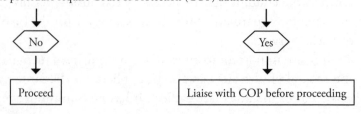

Figure 6.1 Flow chart for assessing capacity

Summary

The management of most day-to-day health issues in people with LD who lack capacity is not complicated and should not, if the person is treated with respect and common sense prevails, pose significant problems for the carers and professionals. In more complicated areas of health care there are now clear guidelines and legal frameworks in place to support decision making processes, which protect people with LD, their carers, relatives and professionals alike.

The key for carers and professionals alike is to always keep the best interests of a person with learning disability at the centre of things, supporting good communication, facilitating discussion and ensuring clear decision making processes. Awareness of the law and the resources available to help decision making should improve access to timely and appropriate health care for people with learning disability, which has on occasions been denied them.

Associated Conditions and Issues

Chapter 7

Epilepsy

Epilepsy is the most common medical condition affecting people with LD. Approximately 1 per cent of the general population suffers with this condition, but for people with LD, particularly those with severe degrees of disability, the figure can be as high as 30–40 per cent. Epilepsy is a condition caused by abnormal electrical 'firing' (chemical/electrical activity) of neurones, which are the nerve cells in the grey matter of the brain. Abnormal, or uncontrolled, firing of these cells triggers 'seizures'.

There are various types of epilepsy and it can manifest in a variety of ways, depending on in which part(s) of the brain the abnormal electrical activity arises, and whether it stays localised to one brain area (partial seizures), or spreads out across the whole brain (generalised seizures) – see below. Partial seizures occur without loss of consciousness. Generalized seizures always cause loss of consciousness.

'Tonic-clonic' seizures are what most people recognise as 'epilepsy'. These affect the whole brain. The patient loses consciousness, goes very stiff, falls to the floor, jerks and twitches, and then comes round after a period of time. Frequently they are incontinent of urine, may bite their tongue and often injure themselves. If a seizure arises in just a part of the brain controlling muscle function (primary motor cortex) the only sign may be twitching of a limb. If the seizure arises in the back of the brain, where vision is interpreted, visual hallucinations may be experienced. In other parts of the brain, other manifestations, such as aggressive behaviour or confusion, may be features. The idea that epilepsy is always associated with loss of consciousness is not true.

At the current time it is well recognised that epilepsy, although the most common neurological condition, is also one of the least well managed. This may be because of the historical stigma associated with the condition, as well as a lack of well-organised services.

There is no consistent model of epilepsy care across Britain, or elsewhere in the world. Currently the majority of sufferers are treated by general practitioners. A minority, mainly those with more complex seizures that have not responded to GP treatment, are seen by neurologists. Some people are seen by general physicians, some by clinical geneticists and some (particularly those who have had head injuries) by doctors specialising in rehabilitation medicine.

Today, there is a growing trend towards people with LD and epilepsy being managed by learning-disability psychiatrists, who, in addition to their knowledge of people with LD, are also trained in the management of epilepsy. This growing trend is due to the following reasons:

- LD and epilepsy may have the same cause (e.g. anoxia during birth, head injury in infancy, genetic metabolic disorders, such as phenylketonuria, cerebral vascular anomalies, etc.).

- Epilepsy may result in brain damage, and make LD worse (e.g. anoxia during seizure, head injury on falling).

- People with LD are at higher risk of accidents, head injury and epilepsy as a consequence.

- Anti-epileptic drugs can cause sedation, and further reduce effective cognitive functions.

- Thus, epilepsy treatment may result in mental deterioration in the patient, and consequent distress and behavioural problems.

- Medications for mental illness (particularly anti-psychotics and some antidepressants) may increase the severity and frequency of seizures.

- Epilepsy may be associated with mental illness in people with LD (as well as others). The mental illnesses associated with epilepsy are divided into 'pre-ictal', 'post-ictal' and 'inter-ictal' illness, depending on the time-relationship to the seizures. They are then further divided into affective, psychotic, neurotic, etc., depending on symptoms and presentation. Relationships between epilepsy and mental illness are complex, and neither should be treated in isolation.

Given the complexity of the relationship between epilepsy, mental illness, behaviour and the medication used to treat the conditions in people with a learning disability, it is always best if one clinician can deal with all aspects of the clinical presentation, otherwise the risks of treating one problem at the expense of making another worse will always exist.

For people with very poorly controlled epilepsy there are also a number of national centres for both children and adults, where they can go and stay for longer periods of time, and have their treatment optimised.

How to support people with learning disabilities and epilepsy

Table 7.1 provides some useful advice about the different challenges that can arise when caring for someone with LD who also has epilepsy.

Table 7.1 Overcoming challenges to managing epilepsy in people with LD

Challenge	Suggestions
Use of multiple medicines	Easy-to-read dosing charts, available from the epilepsy specialist nurse or online
Complex information about medication	Easy-to-read medication information, support in meetings with doctor
Variable response to treatment	Keep records, use seizure diaries
Sensitivity to side-effects	Good awareness of medicines and monitoring
Seizures that may be subtle and therefore hard to detect	Training on what seizures look like
Other LD problems that look like seizures (e.g. autistic behaviours)	Training on other conditions that mimic seizures
May need 'rescue' medication (medication given under specific defined circumstances in addition to regular medication, e.g. following a prolonged seizure or a cluster of small seizures). Training in its use and the protocols associated with its administration will be required for care staff.	Training in use/protocols
Underlying brain damage/genetic disorder	Understanding underlying problems
Physical illness may trigger seizures	Watch for constipation, urinary infection, etc.
Activity overload/under-stimulation may affect seizures, e.g. someone with a learning disability who is over-stimulated may experience high levels of anxiety, which can trigger seizures	Well-managed activities (those appropriate in nature and content to the level of learning disability in question)

Type of seizure

As mentioned above, seizures are categorised into different types and there are a number of classification systems used in the world, although the most commonly used in the UK is the International

League against Epilepsy's system (ILAE). Following the classification of seizure type, different types of seizures occurring together are sometimes further classified into epilepsy 'syndromes'. This type of analysis is often difficult to carry out in people with learning disabilities, especially those with more severe disabilities, who are unable to give a history of their experience prior to and during a seizure. They may also experience different types of seizures at different times.

The reason it is important to define the type of seizure occurring is not simply academic. There are important practical implications. Some seizure types respond better to certain drugs than others, and it is recognised that certain treatments can worsen, rather than help, some types of seizures.

Although the primary aim of treatment is, ideally, to stop seizures completely in people with LD, this is not, unfortunately, always possible. The seizures may, for example, be very resistant to treatment, or the amount of medicine needed to completely stop the seizures may be intolerable or toxic to the patient. Therefore, the focus of treatment may sometimes have to be limited to reducing the severity and frequency of certain types of seizures. It is especially important to control those seizures associated with risk of injury, an example being an atonic seizure, or 'drop attack', where a person suddenly falls to the floor, having lost their body muscle-tone. These seizures are often associated with quite severe facial or head injuries.

The focus of treatment may be to prevent seizures where possible, but also, where some seizures still occur, to minimise injuries in other ways, such as by providing a helmet to protect the patient from injuring his head. Tonic-clonic seizures are also associated with injury, or, in some cases, even death, and the importance of seizure-control in these cases cannot be over-emphasised.

What can you do to help support a client with epilepsy?

Diagnosis

It is commonly believed that there is a specific test for epilepsy, particularly the electro-encephalogram – also described as the 'EEG' or 'brainwave trace'. However, this is not always a reliable diagnostic test. In Table 7.2 there is a description of the range of diagnostic tools that are used. (Remember to check the glossary for any terms unfamiliar to you.)

Table 7.2 Tests used in management of epilepsy

Test	Application
EEG (Electroencephalogram/'brainwave trace')	Can look at brainwave activity at a point in time (over a 30 minute period) or if the recording is carried out over a longer period e.g. 24–48 hours it may be possible to tie in abnormalities of the brainwave activity with observable events such as movements or changes in conscious level and behaviour.
Blood tests	To check medication levels/monitor health, as medications may conceal a physical health problem
ECG (electrocardiograph/'heart trace')	Exclude cardiac problems leading to 'fits', e.g. cardiac ischaemia, arrhythmias
Witness descriptions	This is the only truly diagnostic tool – two witnessed seizures are needed to diagnose epilepsy
Video	It is helpful to see actual seizures
Video-telemetry	Combined video with an EEG (often done overnight in hospital) Can see an actual seizure, and an EEG trace, together on a split-screen.

It's worth remembering that people may still have epilepsy while having a normal surface EEG. A very abnormal EEG does not necessarily mean the subject has epilepsy either. Epilepsy is primarily a clinical diagnosis, which means it is made on the description by witnesses of what actually happens to the subject during a specific event. This is not to say that EEG is not useful in identifying from which area of the brain the epilepsy is originating.

Also, in people where there is no clinical seizure activity, very disturbed EEGs showing a lot of sub-clinical seizure activity can be associated with subtle behavioural or cognitive difficulties. This can improve with the use of anti-epileptic drugs.

When taking a person with LD to an appointment for epilepsy, ideally the accompanying carer should have themselves witnessed what happened when the 'epileptic seizure' occurred. Also, if the witness cannot attend, the person who does go with the patient should take an accurate written account of what was seen. This is particularly important when the question of epilepsy is being raised for the first time. Given the fact that seizures present in a variety of ways, a number of descriptions are recognised for different types of seizures. Notable, however, is the fact that the seizure pattern is usually the same each time in any individual, which is helpful in making a diagnosis.

Below is a seven-point list of details which, if epilepsy is suspected, are worth recording prior to an appointment. Even if the epilepsy is years old, and it's a follow up appointment, the following information is useful to take along:

1. Detailed **description** of the event(s)

2. **Diary** of all similar events, frequency, duration and any other factors which may be relevant, such as where they occur, what time of day and, in women, whether there is a relationship to the menstrual cycle

3. List all **medication**, or any other treatment, whether prescription, non-prescription or herbal, that may interact with anti-epileptic drugs or induce seizures

4. Any problems possibly related to **side-effects** of medication, e.g. antipsychotics, and also some antidepressants, can cause seizures, while benzodiazepines have anti-seizure activity

5. Any **injuries** sustained by the victim during seizure activity

6. Details of any physical **health problems** (e.g. constipation, chest or urinary tract infection)

7. What people are like **after the seizure**, e.g. sleepy, confused, agitated, aggressive, appearing to hallucinate, etc.

Epilepsy and medication

Below is a list of medication commonly prescribed for the different forms of epilepsy. This is followed by Table 7.3 showing associated side-effects of the drugs (although not necessarily in relation to someone who has epilepsy).

- *Carbamazepine*: Used for primary and secondary generalised seizures, some primary generalised seizures.

- *Benzodiazepines* (Diazepam, Clonazepam): Status epilepticus, febrile convulsions, convulsions due to poisoning.

- *Sodium Valproate* (Epilim): All forms of epilepsy.

- *Lamotrigine* (Lamictal): Monotherapy and adjunctive treatment of partial seizures and primary and secondary generalised tonic-clonic seizures, and seizures associated with Lennox-Gastaut Syndrome.

- *Gabapentin* (Neurontin): Adjunctive treatment of partial seizures with/without secondary generalisation, not adequately controlled with other anti-epileptics. Not much used these days.

- *Leviteracetam* (Keppra): Monotherapy and adjunctive treatment of partial seizures with/without secondary generalisation, and adjunctive therapy for myoclonic seizures.

- *Topiramate* (Topamax): Monotherapy and adjunctive treatment of generalised tonic-clonic seizures or partial seizures with/without secondary generalisation; adjunctive treatment in seizures in Lennox-Gastaut Syndrome.

- *Phenytoin* (Epanutin): All forms of epilepsy, except absence seizures (characterised by brief losses of awareness). Old-fashioned.

- *Phenobarbitone*: All forms of epilepsy, except absence seizures. Not used except in rare cases where all else fails.

Table 7.3 Commonly used anti-epileptic drugs and their potential for causing side-effects

Drug	Summary of side-effects (see medication leaflets for full details)
Carbamazepine (Tegretol)	Dizziness, double vision, unsteadiness, nausea and vomiting, slowed thinking
Benzodiazepines: Clobazam (Clobazam); Clonazepam (Rivotril); Diazepam (Valium)	Sedation, respiratory problems (increase), rarely dis-inhibition/irritability
Sodium Valproate (Epilim)	Tremors, weight gain, irritability, confusion, gastric intolerance
Lamotrigine (Lamictal)	Rash (in which case stop drug), alexia, double vision, vomiting (dose dependent), sedation, insomnia
Gabapentin (Neurontin)	Upset stomach, tissue swelling, dizziness, drowsiness, tremor, abnormal walk, forgetfulness, weight gain, slurring speech, joint pains, double vision, confusion, shortness of breath, tingling, depression, psychosis, headache
Levetiracetam (Keppra)	Sedation, slurred speech, slowed thinking, weight loss, tingling, mental health problems
Topiramate (Topamax)	Sedation, unsteadiness*, slurred speech*, nausea*, vomiting* (* = overdose)
Phenytoin (epanutin)	Sedation, unsteadiness, slurred speech, slowed thinking, coarsening of skin
Phenobarbitone (less commonly used now)	Very many side-effects, toxic, not used much nowadays

Rescue medication

Some people with LD who have epilepsy are prescribed additional 'rescue medication' in addition to their regular medication regime. Rescue medication is used in two main circumstances. The first is for protracted seizure activity.

PROTRACTED SEIZURE ACTIVITY

In most people the brain's in-built mechanisms stop seizures after one or two minutes. In some people these mechanisms do not appear to work, and when they have a seizure it can continue for much longer periods. Sometimes seizures will not stop without medical intervention ('*status epilepticus*').

Prolonged seizures are recognised not only to cause possible brain damage, but also to place people at a great risk of a cardiac or respiratory arrest. These events are rare, but may be predisposed to by other factors, such as inter-current physical illness. In such emergencies, it is appropriate to call a 999 ambulance. Paramedics are trained in the administration of both rectal as well as intravenous Diazepam, which will usually stop the seizure.

Undeniably, in a minority of epileptic people with LD, protracted seizures are the 'norm', and it would be impractical to repeatedly call an ambulance, perhaps as often as daily or more. Extra rescue medication can be administered by trained staff, following a planned protocol, after a designated period of seizure activity. At the current time, the main rescue medication that is administered is rectal Diazepam. There are clearly practical and ethical issues about administering a drug by the rectal route, and specific training is required to do it.

Currently other drugs that can be given by alternative routes, are being assessed for their use in terminating prolonged seizures. These include Lorazepam and Midazolam. Both these drugs belong to the same family of drugs as Diazepam (the Benzodiazepines), and can be squirted into the cheek pouches (buccal), or into the nose (nasal). Neither of these drugs is yet licensed for this type of treatment, and although the routes of administration may appear less controversial, than rectal administration the licensing matter has to be borne in mind.

CLUSTER SEIZURES

The second circumstance when rescue medication might be administered is when a person has 'cluster seizures'. Here a seizure is invariably followed by a number of further seizures in a short space of time, perhaps occurring as many as three or four times in a day. Under these circumstances it may again be wise to give additional medication, usually orally, to prevent these clusters occurring. This medication can often be given orally, for a limited period, and a long-acting Benzodiazepine, like Clobazam or Clonazepam, may be a good choice. Again, the administration should be guided by a protocol, an example of which is given in Figure 7.1

Seizure type/s: _____

Usual duration of seizure: _____

After how long or how many seizures should Epistatus* be given?

_____

Initial dose of Epistatus (in mgs) _____

Can a second dose be administered?   No   Yes
    When? (After how long or how many seizures) _____
    Second dose (in mgs) _____

When to call for an ambulance _____

Special instructions (e.g. should procedure be witnessed, situations when Epistatus should not be used)

Signed _____   Date _____

Prescribing Doctor

Figure 7.1 Emergency protocol – with PRN medication protocol for administration

*   Epistatus is a form of Midazolam, which has limited approval

Chapter 8

Sleep Problems

Insomnia (difficulty initiating or maintaining sleep) is a symptom of illness, not an illness itself. It is caused by a variety of external (e.g. environmental) and internal factors (e.g. psychiatric illness, stress, physical illness, medication). There may be problems initiating sleep, waking frequently overnight or waking early in the morning and being unable to get back to sleep. The causes, where possible, should be determined and treated. Sometimes there is one main cause, but often several factors interacting together will cause a sleep disturbance.

It is well recognised that sleep disorders are more common in people with LD, for a number of reasons, including:

- relatively high levels of physical deformity, particularly affecting the face and upper airways

- sensory deficits

- epilepsy with nocturnal seizures

- upper airway obstruction

- high incidence of psychiatric disorders.

Conditions associated with upper airway obstruction include Down's syndrome, Mucopolysaccharidoses, Fragile X syndrome, Prader-Willi syndrome, cerebral palsy, hydrocephalus and

Arnold-Chiari malformation. Obesity is also frequently associated with breathing difficulties.

These causes are in addition to conventional causes of insomnia, which include physical causes (such as hormonal changes in women, medical conditions such as asthma, heart conditions, osteoarthritis or hyperthyroidism); psychological causes (such as anxiety, stress or depression); temporary events or factors (including adjustment sleep disorders, medication, overuse of caffeine); and environmental factors such as noise or uncomfortable temperatures.

Insomnia can also be a sign of an undiagnosed medical or psychological condition. If insomnia persists for more than a few weeks, it's best to see your doctor for an assessment.

The Sleep diary recording sheet in Figure 8.1 is a good way of trying to work out what may be causing the problem.

In general, when people present with a disturbance of sleep without an obvious underlying cause, a programme of 'sleep hygiene' should be tried in the first instance. This includes the following principles:

- Avoid excess caffeine, alcohol or nicotine at least 3 or 4 hours before bed (a hot milky or protein-rich drink at bedtime may promote sleep).

- Don't stay in bed for prolonged periods of time if not asleep. Go to another dimly lit room; ensure the bedroom is primarily used for sleeping.

- Avoid daytime naps or long periods of inactivity.

- A warm bath or exercise a few hours before bedtime may promote sleep.

- Do not engage in strenuous physical exertion or mental activity immediately prior to bedtime, as this can inhibit sleep.

- Make sure the bed and bedroom are as comfortable as possible, avoiding extremes of noise, temperature and humidity.

Sleep Diary
Name:
Week Commencing:

	Monday	Tuesday	Wednesday	Thursday	Friday	Saturday	Sunday
Time woke in the morning							
Mood on waking							
Time of nap(s) in day							
Time went to bed in evening							
Time went to sleep in the evening							
Time(s) woke in night							
What you did?							
Time(s) went to sleep again							
Time you went to bed							

Figure 8.1 Sleep diary

- Establish a regular routine at bedtime (i.e. go to bed at the same time and rise at the same time every morning).

- Carbohydrates (e.g. pasta, etc.) help sleep, but avoid large meals within two hours of going to bed. Food rich in refined sugars may inhibit sleep, as may some vitamin preparations.

- A number of prescribed medications inhibit sleep. If suspected, prescriptions should be reviewed.

Medication for sleep

Assuming 'sleep hygiene' is good, hypnotic or sleep-inducing drugs should only be used sparingly, and for short periods. They can be very helpful when someone's sleep and wake cycles have become disturbed (e.g. they are awake at night and asleep during the daytime). This can be quite easily rectified by the judicious and timely use of hypnotic medication. For example, if someone needs to be asleep by midnight instead of 2.00 am, the hypnotic can be given 5 minutes earlier each night, taking 12 days to change each hour of the sleep-wake cycle.

In some people with LD, particularly with genetic syndromes associated with severe degrees of disability, there appears to be an underlying defect in the mechanisms in the brain that initiate and maintain sleep.

In such cases it is sometimes worth trying melatonin. Melatonin is a hormone found in the brain, which plays an important role in inciting and maintaining sleep. It is also available in synthetic form as a medication, which can be administered as a hypnotic. When taken as medication there are few side-effects and no 'hangover', unlike many conventional hypnotics, which are mostly based on Benzodiazepines (Valium-type drugs). Given that Melatonin is currently unlicensed in the UK, it may only be possible to obtain it from specialists (e.g. consultants). Although this medication is currently not licensed for use in the UK, it is available over-the-counter in many parts of the world, including the USA. It is often recommended for jet lag, and is viewed as relatively safe. The only possible contraindication is epilepsy. In many people who have long-standing disturbance of sleep, particularly in initiating sleep, Melatonin can be very helpful. The usual dose is 5mg at first, taken about 20 minutes before retiring.

If Melatonin is not helpful, other hypnotics are available, such as Zopiclone (Zimovane), which is not associated with some of the hangover effects of the Benzodiazepines. In really resistant cases Benzodiazepines (e.g. Temazepam) still have a part to play, as do other hypnotics such as Heminevrin or Chloral hydrate. However, before any hypnotic medication is considered, all reasonable causes of sleep disturbance need to be excluded.

Chapter 9
Swallowing Problems

Problems with swallowing are more common in people with LD than in the general population. The medical term for this condition is 'dysphagia'. However, this is a *symptom* of a problem, and not a condition in its own right. There are two main causes of swallowing difficulties:

- a mechanical or structural blockage anywhere between the mouth and stomach

- a neurological problem affecting either the power or coordination of the muscles involved in swallowing.

In general, neurological problems are the main cause of swallowing difficulties seen in people with a learning disability. They often relate to underlying brain dysfunction. These problems occur in some people with moderate to severe degrees of disability, rather than in those with mild disability.

Signs of a swallowing problem include:

- reluctance to eat

- dribbling saliva

- coughing or choking on eating

- turning blue when eating

- recurrent chest infections
- regurgitation of food
- unexplained weight loss
- pain on swallowing/sensation of food getting stuck
- other signs of malnutrition.

Why recognising a swallowing problem is important

In an acute situation a swallowing problem can cause choking, and, on occasions, death, if the trachea or a major airway is blocked and leads to respiratory arrest. Fortunately, this situation is relatively rare. It is much more common for small amounts of liquid or food to 'go down the wrong way' i.e. instead of going down the oesophagus (gullet) into the stomach, food goes into the lungs. This usually shows itself by recurrent chest infections, which often respond poorly to antibiotics. It can progress to pneumonia, and eventually lead to long-term irreversible deterioration in lung function.

What are the causes?

In regard to mechanical causes of dysphagia, anything blocking the passage of food between the mouth and the stomach can cause problems. These include cleft lip and palate, abscesses in the mouth, throat or thorax, severe tonsillitis, pharyngeal pouches (little swellings on the side of the upper gullet where food can accumulate), tumours of the tongue, thorax or oesophagus, or the upper part of the stomach. Also, any enlargement of organs or glands within the chest where the oesophagus passes through can also lead to difficulties swallowing. Gastro Oesophageal Reflux Disease (GORD) is very common in PWLD and stomach acid can cause scarring.

Neurological causes can be difficulties within the brain, the nerve supply to the muscles or the muscles themselves (e.g. cerebral palsy, stroke and Parkinsons Disease). Given the complexity of swallowing, with the large number of muscles involved, anything affecting coordination of muscle activity can lead to swallowing problems. In people with learning disabilities the most common cause is difficulties within the brain, and particularly the parts of the brain involved in muscle coordination. However, other factors can cause swallowing problems indirectly, the most common being medication, particularly drugs that suppress central brain function, such as Benzodiazepines (e.g. Diazepam), drugs that cause conditions called dystonias (e.g. drugs used to treat vomiting and sickness, or some mental health problems) and drugs effecting muscular contraction. These problems are easily reversible if the medication is stopped.

Managing and treating a swallowing problem

The management of dysphagia depends on the underlying cause, and so an initial assessment into that is imperative. Discovering the cause of dysphagia is vital, as in many cases reversible factors may be discovered, enabling an easy remedy.

If the cause of dysphagia is mechanical (i.e. a blockage somewhere), then often the treatment is surgical. However, in most cases the problem is neurological, and in these situations there is sometimes a specific neurological condition that may respond to treatment (e.g. withdrawing a medication giving side effects, treating Parkinsons disease, using botulinum toxin). If the neurological condition does not have a specific treatment, then modifications to the consistency of the diet (e.g. liquidising solid foods or adding thickeners to liquid to make swallowing easier) may help in the first instance. Providing advice in this area is a particular function of speech and language therapists and/or dieticians.

If the swallowing is very poor then it may be necessary to feed the subject through a fine feeding-tube introduced via the nose (Nasogastric tube). If the problem is thought to be relatively short-term this is the preferred route. If long-term feeding is required then a Percutaneous Endoscopic Gastrostomy 'PEG' feed tube can be fitted directly into the stomach.

Chapter 10

Autism

There is often confusion about what is meant by the term 'autism', and whether it means the same as 'learning disability'. This arises because approximately 70 per cent of people with autism also have a significant degree of learning disability with an IQ below 70. However, 30 per cent of autistic people have normal or above average levels of intellectual ability. Autism is primarily a developmental disorder, in which there are difficulties in three core areas of life.

These are:

- impairment in social interaction
- impairment in communication
- restrictive imagination or repetitive behaviours.

People with autism have different degrees of impairment in the different areas, and so consequently very few people with autism are exactly alike. It is best to look at the range of behaviours in people on the 'autistic spectrum', by considering each feature separately.

Impairment in social interaction

Included in impairment in social interaction are three types of behaviour, primarily described in children (although similar patterns of behaviour are seen in adults).

1. Some autistic people are described as 'aloof'. They tend not to interact spontaneously, and may even actively resist approaches by other people. They tend not to speak or to use non-verbal communication such as gesture, eye contact or sign language. They are often 'tactile defensive', not liking to be touched or held. They don't seek comfort when distressed, and find any human contact distressing or anxiety provoking. Such people may become physically aggressive if their personal space is invaded. This level of social impairment is seen at the more severe end of the autistic spectrum, and is often associated with significant degrees of learning disability.

2. Other autistic people are described as 'passive'. They do not actively resist social contact, but neither do they actively seek it out. They often respond to questions and answer appropriately, but are not particularly interested in conversation. Social interaction is simply part of the daily routine, but on the whole they tend to be fairly indifferent about it.

3. There is a third group who can be described as 'active but odd'. These people actually want to interact with people, and will make spontaneous approaches, but because they do not understand the rules of social behaviour, their interactions may be very one-sided. They may ask inappropriate or personal questions, make physical contact with strangers on the street or talk to someone about a particular interest they have without picking up on the signs that the person has heard enough, and have no further interest in discussing the topic. This type of social impairment is seen more at the able end of the spectrum, in which people are often described as having Asperger's syndrome or 'high-functioning autism'. This type of social interaction can be problematic, as others often misinterpret these odd approaches, and they can even result, on occasions, in police involvement. Examples are touching or invading personal space.

Thus while some people with autism are totally withdrawn, many interact but in an unusual way compared with others of their age or level of learning disability. Other social impairments seen in people with autistic spectrum disorder are unusual types of eye contact (people with autism often will not look others in the eye).

They often have problems in taking turns, and butt in to group conversation before others have finished speaking. They have problems waiting for their turn in games, and have a lack of joint attention (i.e. showing things to people simply to share interest with them). They may also demonstrate a lack of empathy, shown by not reacting with concern if someone is hurt, for example. Each of these impairments relates to a lack of understanding of the basic social rules that govern the way that people interact on a day-to-day basis. Without understanding these impairments, it is easy to view people with autism as being rude or insensitive.

Impairment in communication

Approximately 50 per cent of people who are diagnosed with autism are functionally mute, that is they do not use spoken language at all to communicate.

There is some evidence that they may in fact understand spoken language. For those who do have spoken language, their use of words is often unusual. They often repeat back phrases that they have heard before, often copying the accent of the speaker and using the same intonation. This is called 'echolalia'. Some repeat the last few words that somebody has said, or it can be a delayed phenomenon, with repetition of favourite phrases from films or adverts, etc. Some may use only this type of communication. They may appear to be holding a reasonable conversation, but when broken down into its components only a number of set phrases are used over and over again, often in a relatively appropriate fashion, but without real meaning.

Autistic people often have problems in understanding the social context of language, or why we ever speak to each other at all. This is an area called 'pragmatics'. Consequently, an autistic person may be asked to carry out a task, and may respond 'yes' but then not actually carry out the task requested. This can lead to confusion about someone's abilities, rather than recognition that they do not understand the social significance of language.

People with autistic spectrum disorder often interpret words very literally, which makes the understanding of metaphor, sarcasm and irony very difficult for them. This makes it necessary that any instructions or comments made to people with autism be given in very clear and simple ways, without the use of the complex and rich language in common everyday communication. Sentences have to be short, and without the use of double negatives, etc. People with autism often mix up pronouns, e.g. 'I' for 'you', or 'they' for 'us'.

The use of non-verbal communication may also be impaired, so people with autism do not tend to back up what they are saying with the usual gestures, such as nodding or shaking their heads when saying yes or no, or pointing to an object when asking someone for it. Equally, they have problems interpreting the facial expressions of others, and often fail to pick up anger or annoyance.

They also have limited abilities to interpret tone and instructions. Therefore some people with autism may not speak at all, and may not have any form of non-verbal communication either. Other people may be highly fluent in their speech and come across as virtually normal, but sometimes display echolalia, take thing too literally or fail to understand pragmatics. The range of communication impairments can therefore be as great as that seen in social impairment.

Restrictive imagination and repetitive behaviours

It is often said that children with autism do not become particularly involved in imaginative play, for example, although they will play with toys, they do not make up stories about them, just line them up in rows, and become very distressed if the lines are disturbed. They may become very interested in one component of a toy, such as spinning the wheel on a toy train. Their play might become very repetitive, and children, as well as adults, can be particularly obsessed with a particular video or film. They will often be able to repeat large chunks of the dialogue. They may develop obsessive interest in specific topics, such as certain cartoon characters, or inanimate objects, such as car-exhaust pipes, and form unusual attachments to particular objects, such as pieces of chain or string.

As with the other difficulties already described, the range of possible behaviours seen within this category is very wide, and varies depending on the levels of intellectual ability. Consequently, an adult with autism and associated severe learning disability may spend a lot of their time rocking and flapping their hands, twirling a piece of string or tearing up magazines. They may scream and cry if their routine is disturbed. Something as minor as their transport from their day centre using a different route due to a traffic diversion may be enough to cause a massive and catastrophic temper tantrum, associated with physical aggression on their return home. On the other hand, a person with high-functioning autism or Asperger's syndrome may be working as a professor at a university and have world-wide recognition as an expert in a relatively obscure field!

Cognitive profiles

Most people with autism have typically uneven cognitive abilities. This means that regardless of the level of learning disability, someone with an autistic spectrum disorder often has things that they are very good at, and others at which they are very poor (although this is, to a certain degree, normal within the general population). Some people are better at maths than English, some have better memories for names, some for routes on maps, etc.

In people with autistic spectrum disorder, these peaks and troughs tend to be more exaggerated. Sometimes the peaks are so great that the person is viewed as having a 'savant ability'. This usually encompasses having amazing memory for detail, such as that of seeing a scene, or a picture, only for a brief period of time, but then being able to copy it in great detail. Others have calendrical mathematical abilities and are able to work out the days of the week for any given year within seconds. However, only about 10 per cent of autistic people have any such abilities.

Causes of autism

The diagnosis of autism is based on a series of behaviours that occur together, leading to impairment in social functioning, communication and imagination, as previously described. However, at the current time the cause of the condition is unknown. It is recognised that a wide range of genetic conditions are associated with the diagnosis, including Fragile X syndrome and tuberous sclerosis, both conditions that are also normally associated with learning disabilities. Thus, when people with autistic disorders are diagnosed, it is purely on what behaviours they present, and, most usually, their levels of cognitive abilities, and the underlying cause or aetiology of the disorder, is not often known.

Autism is often described in a number of ways, which leads to confusion. For someone to be diagnosed as autistic they must show impairment in the three core features of the condition (social, communication and imagination), and these impairments must have been present in the child before the age of 3. If these problems arise later in life, perhaps in adulthood, they may be indicative of other conditions, such as degenerative brain disorder, or the onset of mental illness.

Sometimes autistic people do not display problems in all three areas to the same severity, and may only have minimal difficulties – an example being repetitive behaviours. In these situations it is possible that the diagnosis of 'atypical autism' will be made. Other diagnoses that are sometimes seen are Asperger's syndrome and high-functioning autism. Both these conditions suggest that the person does not have an associated learning disability. It must be remembered, however, that anyone with a diagnosis of autistic spectrum disorder should have clear evidence of difficulties in the three areas described.

Why is it important to recognise the condition

Although there is no specific medical treatment for autism, it is important to recognise when a person with learning disability is suffering from the condition, in order to be able to ensure that the environment in which they live is appropriate for their needs. People with LD and autism are often prone to behavioural difficulties, and research has shown that many people with so-called 'challenging behaviour' are in fact autistic, and that the environment in which they live or work is not appropriate.

Although it is now more common for people to be diagnosed with autism in early childhood, there are still many adults living within the community in whom the diagnosis has not been made, despite a long history of disturbed behaviour, including physical aggression or self-injurious behaviour. In these situations, changes of environment can bring about significant improvements.

Below are some lists of behaviours indicating that a person with a learning disability may be autistic (suggested by Dr Steve Hinder and reproduced here with his permission).

Social interaction

In relation to social interaction, they:

- may show little eye contact, or engage in inappropriate staring
- may withdraw from any kind of interaction
- interact better with staff (predictable) than peers (unpredictable)
- may want to join in with others, but lack the skills to do so, and end up on the outside looking in at the activities of others
- may have poor understanding of gestures, and failure to pick up on social cues
- may have trouble with interpreting facial expressions
- may hardly seem to notice peers
- may have difficulty putting themselves in someone else's shoes
- clients with autism are often socially aloof, or passive, but a large 'active but odd' subgroup have a drive to be sociable. They may be unaware of how to initiate appropriate social interaction – they may be overly aggressive or boisterous when trying to join in with others
- never really develop friendships or understand the true meaning of affection
- do not turn to look at what a carer is looking at (shared attention/gaze)
- rarely point to indicate a need, or a thing of interest
- may have episodes of going 'blank', or retreating into own world/shell for a few seconds, or several minutes

- may pull by hand/push another adult towards a desired object
- often do not understand the meaning behind a simple event or perception, e.g. will see water drops running down the outside of a window, but will not conclude that it is likely to be raining outside
- have little understanding of social rules/boundaries/ conventions – this can often lead to social *faux pas*, or behaviours which cause embarrassment to others
- may want to be affectionate, but only at specific times and on own terms
- show little reaction to the needs or distress of others
- engage only in one-sided interaction, with no to-and-fro
- may only engage socially to get something he/she wants
- often seem uninterested in what others think of them – they will not seek praise or recognition after achieving something, and will not spontaneously bring things to show other people, e.g. objects, art work
- have an apparent lack of spontaneity, with cues/prompting required for every activity – this may be interpreted as poor motivation
- if upset, can often be comforted without any true two-way interaction taking place (i.e. the carer might as well be an object, no eye contact involved)
- don't initiate social actions, or produce them spontaneously (e.g. waving goodbye).

Communication

Remember:

- clients with autism are often completely non-verbal
- though many clients with profound learning disability are also non-verbal, those with autism are less likely to

compensate with appropriate gestures, facial expression, body language, etc.

- if Makaton/signing is used, it is often in a rigid or repetitive way

- if gesturing is used, it may be purely functional, rather than expressing feelings

- may appear 'wooden' when communicating/interacting i.e. stiff, arms by side, little movement or facial expression

- may make frequent involuntary noises – grunts, groans, whistles, clicks, squeals

- little understanding of the rules of conversation – if non-verbal, will interrupt the conversation of others if in need

- understanding and ability to follow instructions may be far better than amount of speech. However, this may not be true understanding, and the individual may be picking up on cues/routines

- may take things very literally, and not understand negatives or paradoxical intentions, e.g. will respond by action or speech in a concrete way to 'You do that again and… ', 'Can you bring that to me?', or 'Would you like to tidy up?' (i.e. they will carry out undesired behaviour again, or answer yes and no respectively)

- information processing may be incredibly slow – it is sometimes worth waiting at least 30 seconds for a client with autism to reply to a question or respond to a request

- if speech is present, it is often unusual in character (stilted, monotonous, pedantic, strange accent)

- there are usually severe problems with appropriate turn-taking skills

- tendency to talk 'at' people rather than 'with' them

- clients may prefer to whisper, or respond well if whispered to

- often mix up pronouns, such as he/she, and may refer to self as 'you', or by own name rather than using the word 'I'

- echolalia – repeating, parrot fashion, the last word or a whole phrase just spoken by someone else. This can be delayed, e.g. repeating a phrase from a TV programme, out of context, months after it was heard

- repetitive speech/questioning, often hundreds of times. This can include catchphrases from TV/video, which are repeated with exact intonation, showing good mimickry skills. The topic is often an obsession for the client.

Need for sameness, obsessions and stereotyped or ritualistic behaviour

- insist on sameness

- get upset/anxious if normal routine is changed

- may be fascinated with a particular object/toy, and carry it around

- objects are used in a repetitive way, with little imagination

- clients may be perfectionists, unable to tolerate making mistakes in their work. Sometimes, if something is broken accidentally, it then has to be smashed completely – everything is black or white, good or bad

- little understanding of make-believe/role play

- need for structure and routine

- future events need to be carefully signposted, and activities broken into simple steps

- may become engrossed in one activity, often repetitive, for hours on end

- play, games and activities are often solitary, repetitive, stereotyped and lacking in creativity

- may take apart mechanical/electrical things

- destruction of objects

- if verbal, may have one particular main topic of conversation all the time

- repetitive, ritualistic behaviours e.g. turning taps/switching lights on and off, touching/tapping surfaces, tearing paper, flushing toilet, spinning objects, hand-washing, lining things up in rows
- fascination with twirling own hands
- rapidly flicking pages of magazines
- over-precise, liking things to be 'just so' – e.g. everything has its rightful place, would notice if object moved, must use certain utensil, must take certain route in car
- whole-body spinning or twirling movements
- hand-flapping when excited
- if interrupted in an activity, may have to start at the beginning again
- may be unusual rituals – e.g. having to kiss floor before passing through door, having to retrace steps
- may become completely 'frozen' or stuck during a physical activity
- may adopt odd body positions and postures for long periods of time
- finger flicking
- may make repetitive noises or sounds, e.g. humming, squealing
- may be facial/body tics and involuntary movements, grimacing
- rocking.

Sensory features

- react with anxiety to certain specific noises, or loud, sudden noise (e.g. dog barking, hoover, lawnmower, traffic, sirens, drills)
- may cover ears with hands

- may be distracted by tuning into background noise, e.g. electrical hum of TV, extractor fan, buzzing insects, wind

- anxiety in crowded, noisy places

- can ignore very loud noises, but react quickly or tune into a specific quiet noise, such as a crisp-packet opening, or conversation in the next room

- may expose himself/herself to very loud noise, such as placing ear to speaker, and then appear to 'shut down', and become oblivious to outside stimuli

- may be fascinated by the way in which light shines/reflects on objects – e.g. spinning top, mirror, sunlight on water, Christmas lights

- general fascination for things that sparkle, shimmer, shine

- may pick out and be preoccupied by detail, such as speck of dust, crumb on floor, pattern in carpet/wallpaper, specific irrelevant bit of book/toy/object

- may be over-stimulated, aroused or scared by certain colours, such as red and yellow

- there may be difficulty with transitions and thresholds, e.g. from carpet to lino

- can be distressed by fluorescent lights

- may be fascinated with, or have hatred of, certain textures, such as woollen clothes, labels in clothes, sand, grass, clay, fur

- may enjoy swinging, hanging, rough and tumble, fairground rides

- may love certain forms of vibration, such as speaker, washing machine, particular vehicles

- frequently have a huge love of music, and may communicate better through rhythm

- often a huge love of water, splashing about

- little sense of temperature

- may seem not to feel pain, appearing not to react to severe injury
- may try to take off own clothes frequently, especially shoes and socks, as they feel excruciatingly uncomfortable – over sensitive to light touch
- may seek out deep pressure, e.g. may crawl under cushions/mats, want to sleep in lycra clothing, try to 'cocoon' themselves
- may love massage
- either love or hate sensory rooms
- mouthing of objects
- may smell, sniff or lick people and objects inappropriately
- may only eat foods with a certain texture, e.g. mushy, soft, crunchy
- may be extremely anxious with certain smells (e.g. perfume, faeces, chemicals, tobacco)
- may be limited to eating bland food, as too sensitive to taste
- may crave strong tastes, as underdeveloped sense of taste – may eat inappropriate things indiscriminately (e.g. soil, grass, paint, plastic, faeces).

Other behaviours or characteristics seen in autism

- head-banging
- skin picking
- eye poking
- biting self and others
- complete lack of a sense of danger
- may not seem to understand different emotions in others, but can be acutely sensitive to the 'vibe' or atmosphere in a room

- may always seem underaroused/excited, or overaroused/excited, with no middle ground
- teeth grinding
- walking on tiptoe
- specific fears/phobias, such as dogs, haircuts, darkness
- skills taught in one context may not be generalised to another setting
- may have an unusually good memory for facts, places etc., and make clever associations
- poor concentration
- high activity levels
- easily bored/frustrated, but also easily overloaded
- problems with waiting, e.g. at traffic lights in car, or standing in a queue
- difficulty with transitions from one setting/activity to another
- enormous appetite – may have huge stools
- enormous thirst often for coffee
- difficulty understanding concepts of time, such as 'in ten minutes', 'tomorrow'
- problems with sequencing events
- too much warning about a future exciting event can lead to a big build-up of anxiety
- may be clumsy, ungainly
- can often react badly if given too much choice, but respond better if given just two concrete choices
- may be able to read very well, but without following the meaning
- do well with picture boards/pictorial timetables

- tend to think concretely, and may only respond to clear, direct, concrete instructions
- difficulty in directing behaviour towards a goal set by others
- may prefer to learn/study without the help of others
- may literally only be able to do one thing at once
- good at jigsaws
- attention to detail/fail to see the big picture.

Caring for someone with a learning disability and autism

Although there is no specific medical treatment for autism, there is increasing evidence that certain medications can help in the management of behavioural disorders often seen in people with autism, probably by reducing arousal and anxiety levels. These include classes of medications like the antipsychotics Risperidone and Haloperidol, SSRI Antidepressants and beta-blockers, such as Propranolol, as well as a wide range of other medication used to treat other psychiatric conditions.

At the current time, however, no medication is in fact licensed to treat autism or the behavioural problems often associated with the condition. Consequently, initiation and monitoring of such medication should be done by a specialist clinician with expertise in the area.

However, unless there are co-morbid psychiatric or physical health conditions that may require treatment in their own right, medication only has a relatively small part to play in the management of people with autism. The mainstay of management primarily involves alterations in environment and communications systems, and adaptations to routines – all of which may reduce anxiety levels and the risk of adverse behavioural problems. Physical aggression, self-injurious behaviour and property damage is discussed below in more detail.

Environment

People with autism, and particularly those with a learning disability, often have a greater requirement for personal space, preferring to be on their own in a room and become distressed if people come as close as 6 ft (or in some cases even greater distances).

On the whole, people with autism find socialising, particularly with strangers, stressful, and therefore there should not be attempts made to 'force' people to socialise. An example would be taking someone to a party or disco, when they have refused to go, believing that it would be 'good for them to mix'. These types of events can sometimes cause outbursts of significant physical aggression due to overwhelming anxiety.

It is important to keep unnecessary change to a minimum. Examples might be trying to keep any staff team as consistent and as small a group as possible, minimising the use of agency staff where possible. Reducing changes to people's rooms such as décor or colour, etc., unless the person is keen for this to happen.

Attention should be paid to the lighting and acoustic quality of the property. People with autism on the whole also have heightened senses, so high levels of light, particularly outside the natural spectrum (e.g. fluorescent lighting), can be distressing. Certain noises, even low level noises such as the hum of a generator or refrigerator, etc., can also cause distress.

Communication

If people with autism use a verbal communication system, then conversation with them should be as simple and clear as possible. It should never involve double negatives (e.g. 'If you don't want to go nowhere we will just stay here', 'are you not unhappy doing that?') sarcasm or irony. Something that is humorous to a carer may be taken literally by a person with autism (e.g. the joke 'did you hear the one about a talking dog…' might cause upset as dogs can't talk, while 'she laughed her head off' might cause extreme anxiety and distress as the person might think it could happen to them!). People with autism often fail to grasp these concepts, and their use can cause misunderstanding. If a person has no verbal communication system, then attempts should be made to enrol the help of a speech and language therapist.

An alternative communication system often allows people with autism to communicate their needs or distresses, which are often the root cause of behavioural problems. If people are able to learn it, then Makaton, a simplified form of sign language, is often useful. In other people, with more severe degrees of disability, object-referencing systems may be developed, i.e. using objects as a means of communication, such as a cup to indicate wanting a drink. On the whole, people with autism tend to process visual information better than written information, and so such things as photo timetables, explaining to people what they will be doing during a day or week, can be extremely useful – particularly for those people who find finishing or starting particular activities difficult.

Routine

Most people enjoy surprises in life and find strict day-to-day routines boring. However, in general, people with autism prefer their life to be as ordered and predictable as possible. They find changes in what they expect to happen stressful and, consequently, to reduce the stress levels, their lives should be as ordered, structured and predictable as possible. If there are any planned changes to a routine, then attempts should always be made to explain this to the person in advance, so that it does not come as a shock.

Clearly it is not possible to control every possible change within a person's life, but change should always be kept to an absolute minimum. This is the reason why people with autism often find times such as holiday or Christmas difficult. Other areas where routines and unpredictability can cause problems are if people like collecting particular objects, which can lead to hoarding behaviour (e.g. books or magazines, or even things such as light bulbs). The person can become distressed or unhappy if their possessions are interfered with, particularly if they are disposed of.

Section 3
Accessing Services

Chapter 11

Screening Programmes

At the current time in the United Kingdom there are a number of health-screening programmes underway, from carrying out blood tests for metabolic disorders in the new-born, to cervical and breast screening programmes in women.

For a health-screening programme to be useful, a number of criteria should be met:

- The illness or disease screened for is relatively common (it's not cost-effective to screen the whole country for illness that affects only ten people a year).

- The cause of disease or final outcome must be significantly changed by treatment if the disease is caught early, even before symptoms are present.

- There must be relatively simple, reliable, cheap and risk-free tests available to detect the disease.

- The process has to be acceptable for people undergoing the programme.

Not surprisingly, given the above criteria, there are not many health conditions routinely screened for in the general population. Table 11.1 below shows some common tests that are useful.

Table 11.1: Screening programmes

Population screening	
Cervical cytology	Diabetes
Breast screening	Colonic cancer
Hypertension	Raised cholesterol
Learning disability – Specific programmes	
Down's syndrome –	e.g. Sensory screening Thyroid Dementia screening Cervical spine instability
Tuberous sclerosis –	Renal scans Specific brain scans
Conditions worth screening for in someone who has a learning disability	
Heliobactor pyloria infection Hepatitis B	Urinary tract infection

In some people, lifestyle or other factors place them at increased risk of particular health problems. An example is someone excessively over-weight (obese), who is at increased risk of diabetes, high cholesterol, cardiovascular disease and stroke. Consequently, a screening programme on people weighing over 15 stone would find a higher than average prevalence of diabetes, high cholesterol and heart disease than it would in people under 10 stone.

In some blood disorders confined to certain racial groups (e.g. sickle-cell anaemia in West Africans), screening outside affected populations will produce no positive results, so testing is not worthwhile.

The same is applicable to people with LD. Many have syndromes caused by chromosomal or genetic problems, often associated with higher risks of specific physical and mental health problems. Therefore, in people with certain syndromes, specialised screening programmes *are* advisable, and have proved to be of benefit. Examples of these are Down's syndrome, which pre-disposes to a number of physical health problems. (The details of such a programme are covered in Box 5.1 in Chapter 5.) and tuberous sclerosis in which many organ systems are affected. The Tuberous Sclerosis Association provides guidelines on what tests should be done. Given the complexity of these, they are usually best carried out in specialist centres.

Chapter 12

Health Checks

It is recommended that people with a learning disability have a 'health check' from time to time. This is more than just a health-screening test. In screening tests the purpose is to pick up relatively common diseases or illnesses early in their course, when treatment is more effective or beneficial. A health check is much more wide ranging, and rather than looking at particular illnesses or diseases, looks at various life-style risks, and even relatively minor health problems that can, in the short or long term, impact on overall well-being and health.

An example is the detection of high blood pressure or hypertension. If left untreated, this leads to increased risk of heart attacks and strokes. Another example is obesity, again leading to increased risk of heart attacks and diabetes. Both conditions are easy to check for, as well as relatively easy to treat or improve, and this can lead to long-term improvement in health and functioning.

Research has shown that many people with learning disabilities and physical-health problems only present to a doctor relatively late on, when their illnesses are quite advanced. For this reason health checks on an annual or biannual basis can be invaluable in preventing long-term ill-health. The following is an example of a health check which the UK government has recommended be carried out on people with a learning disability by their GP. It is called the Cardiff Health Check (or Welsh Health Check) and has been found useful in identifying unrecognised health needs. As can be seen, it is wide-ranging, and its completion should help to cover all the areas in which overt or less easily detectable disorders may exist. This is particularly important in a population that is vulnerable, not only to some illnesses or disorders linked to learning disability, but who also, because of their learning disability, may not be able to describe their symptoms very well, or communicate those complaints properly to those who care for them. It was developed by Professor Mike Kerr at Cardiff University, Wales, and is reproduced here with grateful thanks.

HEALTH CHECK FOR PEOPLE WITH A LEARNING DISABILITY

Date_____   Name_____

Marital Status_____   Ethnic Origin_____

Principal Carer_____   Age_____ Sex____

Address_____

Weight (kg/stone)_____

Height (metres/feet)_____

Blood pressure_____

Urine analysis _____

Smoke (per day)_____

Alcohol (units per week) _____

Body Mass Index (weight in kg/height in m^2)_____

Cholesterol/Serum lipids_____

Immunisation

People with a learning disability should have the same regimes as others and the same contraindications apply (please circle).

Tetanus in last ten years	Yes	No
If no, has tetanus been given?	Yes	No
Has influenza vaccine been given?	Yes	No

Is Hepatitis B status known?   Yes   No
Results?_____

Cervical screen
People with a learning disability have the same indications for cervical cytology as others.

Is a smear indicated?   Yes   No
If yes when was last smear? ___/___/___
When is next due? ___/___/___
What was the result?_____

Mammography
This should be arranged as per local practice.

Has mammogram been performed?   Yes   No

Chronic illness – Does your patient suffer from any chronic illnesses?
Diabetes   Yes   No
Asthma   Yes   No

System enquiry – the answers to these may not be available
Respiratory cough   Yes   No
Haemoptysis   Yes   No
Sputum   Yes   No
Wheeze   Yes   No
Dyspnoea   Yes   No

Cardiovascular system
Chest pains   Yes   No
Swelling of ankles   Yes   No
Palpitations   Yes   No
Postural nocturnal dyspnoea   Yes   No
Cyanosis   Yes   No

Abdominal

Constipation	Yes	No
Weight loss	Yes	No
Diarrhoea	Yes	No
Dyspepsia	Yes	No
Melaena	Yes	No
Rectal bleeding	Yes	No
Faecal incontinence	Yes	No
Feeding problem	Yes	No

C.N.S. – (for epilepsy see later)

Faints	Yes	No
Parasthesia	Yes	No
Weakness	Yes	No
Where?_____		

Genito-urinary

Dysuria	Yes	No
Frequency	Yes	No
Haematuria	Yes	No
Urinary incontinence	Yes	No
If 'Yes' has M.S.U. been done?	Yes	No
Would you consider other investigations?	Yes	No

Gynae

Dysmenorrhoea	Yes	No
Inter-menstrual bleeding	Yes	No
PV discharge	Yes	No
Is patient post-menopausal?	Yes	No
Contraceptives	Yes	No
Other_____		

Epilepsy

	Yes	No

Type of fit_____

Frequency of seizures (fits/month)_____

Over the last year have the fits:

    Worsened   Remained the same   Improved

Anti-epileptic medication:

Name	Dose/Frequency	Levels (if indicated)

Side-effects observed in the patient_____

Behavioural disturbance

Behavioural disturbance in people with a learning disability is often an indicator of other morbidity. For this reason it is important to record it.

Aggression   Yes   No

More than once a month   less than once a month

             very infrequently

Self-injury   Yes   No

More than once a month   less than once a month

             very infrequently

Overactivity   Yes   No

More than once a month   less than once a month

              very infrequently

Other_____

More than once a month   less than once a month

              very infrequently

Physical examination
General appearance

Anaemia   Yes   No

Lymph nodes   Yes   No

Clubbing   Yes   No

Jaundice   Yes   No

Hydration   Yes   No

Cardio-vascular system

Pulse ...beats/min   Blood pressure

Heart sounds   Ankle Oedema   Yes   No

(describe) _____

Respiratory system

Respiratory rate (breaths/min)_____

Breath sounds   Yes   No

Wheeze   Yes   No

Tachypnoea   Yes   No

Additional sounds   Yes   No

(describe) _____

Abdomen

Masses   Yes   No

Liver   Yes   No

Spleen   Yes   No

PR indicated   Yes   No

Results _____

Central nervous system

It is often difficult and not relevant to perform a full neurological examination; however, people with a learning disability are particularly prone to abnormalities in vision, hearing and communication, and so a change in function would suggest further investigation is necessary.

Vision

Normal vision   Minor visual problem   Major visual problem

Is the carer/key worker concerned?   Yes   No

When did the patient last see an optician? ___/___/___

Is there a cataract?   Yes   No

Result of Snellen chart _____

Any other date ___/___/___

Hearing

Normal hearing   Minor hearing problem   Major hearing problem

Is the carer/key worker concerned?	Yes	No
Does he/she wear a hearing aid?	Yes	No
Any wax?	Yes	No
Does your patient see an audiologist?	Yes	No

Other investigation: _____

Communication

Does your patient communicate normally?	Yes	No
Does your patient communicate with aids?	Yes	No
Does your patient have a severe communication problem?	Yes	No
Does your patient see a speech therapist?	Yes	No

Mobility

Is your patient fully mobile?	Yes	No
Is your patient fully mobile with aids?	Yes	No
Is your patient immobile?	Yes	No
Has mobility been assessed?	Yes	No

Dermatology

Any abnormality?	Yes	No

Diagnosis: _____

Breasts

Any lumps?	Yes	No
Any discharge?	Yes	No
Nipple retraction?	Yes	No

Other investigations

Are there any further investigations necessary?	Yes	No

If yes please indicate: _____

Syndrome-specific check

Certain syndromes causing learning disabilities are associated with increased morbidity. For this reason it is important to record:

Is the cause of learning disability known?   Yes   No

If yes, what is it? _____

Has the patient had a chromosomal analysis?   Yes   No

Result? _____

Degree of learning disability: Mild   Moderate   Severe   Profound

Is a formalised IQ test available?   Yes   No

If yes, what were the results? _____

If your patient has Down's syndrome he/she should have a yearly test for hypothyroidism.

Has this been done?   Yes   No

Other medication

Drug	Dose	Side-effects	Level (if indicated)

Chapter 13

When Admission to Psychiatric Care is Required

What follows is a very brief guide to this complex area. For some people with LD there may be times when admission to psychiatric hospital is necessary. In most places in the UK there are specialist psychiatric hospitals especially intended for people with LD, although in other places these people are admitted to 'general' psychiatric units that have some expertise in the field.

Hospital is a very different environment to living at home, or even in a residential home in the community, and so, clearly, having to be admitted there can be a very stressful and distressing experience for some people with LD. This should never be decided upon lightly. Wherever possible, people with LD who have mental health and/or behavioural problems should be treated and assisted to survive in their normal environment.

The treatment and help that people with LD can be given in community settings includes not only input from their usual carers, but also from:

- consultant psychiatrists working in the community
  – outpatient appointments, home visits, liaison with Community Mental Health Teams (CMHT)

- community learning disability nurses (CLDNs) – visits to assess people with LDs, to counsel them, to assist them in accessing community facilities and to liaise with consultant psychiatrists and other members of the CMHT

- general practitioners (GPs) – these can be available at short notice if required by CLDN, other CMHT members, family, carers, etc.

- social worker – their work overlaps considerably with the CLDN's work, but they are also available particularly to assist people with LD with non-medical problems, such as living conditions, advice or help with finances, etc.

- occupational therapists – these professionals are involved in many different aspects of providing structure and meaning to the day for people with LD. This may be through training in activities of daily living; training in and access to educational and recreational activities; assessing the way a person experiences their environment (particularly in autism) called 'sensory processing', plus many other initiatives that help people with LD to access facilities in the community, in order to improve their health and sense of well-being. In these ways OTs assist in the overall treatment package given to people with LD who have mental illness and/or behavioural problems

- workers from other agencies and organisations – in some circumstances, a wide range of other services may be required. Examples could include Community Drug & Alcohol rehabilitation services, Marriage-Guidance Services, Anger-Management Services, Legal Services, Child Protection Services, Local Councils, Housing Agencies, Social Services (apart from the social worker already involved), various charitable organisations (e.g. Mencap, societies for people with particular disorders, e.g. autism, Down's syndrome, etc.)

- specialist doctors in other fields – such as neurologists, endocrinologists, gynaecologists, etc. Sometimes a consultant psychiatrist and/or the GP will need to liaise with doctors in other specialities, and also arrange appointments for the people with LD to be seen by them

- pharmacists with a clinical role. Invaluable advice and assistance with medication can be obtained from these professionals, who, because of their clinical role, tend to be very up to date and knowledgeable about the efficacy, risks and side-effects of psychotropic ('psychiatric') drugs, either given alone, or in combinations.

Why, or when, should a person with LD be admitted to hospital?

Starting from the position that it is best to avoid hospitalisation if there is an alternative option, admission to hospital may be necessary when the person with LD has a mental illness and/or a behavioural disorder that is:

- putting themselves, or others, at risk

- not responding to home treatment

- new to the person with LD and poorly understood; or

- depriving them of access to usual community facilities

- putting their tenancy in jeopardy.

More detail on these conditions are outlined below.

When mental illness puts the person, or others, at risk

This may be because of suicidal or self-harming behaviour, aggression or violence to others, excessive risk-taking, and even such things as having a serious medical condition that is putting the person with LD at grave risk. It may be that is not being managed or treated because the person's mental or behavioural disorder is making it impossible (e.g. acute appendicitis, but the person with LD, John, is psychotic, and is refusing to be seen because he believes doctors intend to kill him).

The Mental Health Act cannot normally be used to enforce medical or surgical treatment. However, where a person's 'disability of mind' is causing a serious and imminent risk, they can be detained under the MHA. In a case such as John's, it is advisable for the hospital to consult its solicitors. The whole area of 'vital' medical or surgical intervention in people with LD, particularly those who also have mental illness, lack capacity and also do not consent to treatment or actively resist it, is contentious (see Chapter 6) and can be the subject of court proceedings.

When a mental illness is not responding

This point is more self-explanatory and refers to those cases when the illness is not responding to treatment/management in the community, despite 'best efforts' of carers, professionals and services.

When a mental illness is new to the person or poorly understood

When mental illness/behavioural disorder is new to the person with LD or poorly understood, it may need a more thorough assessment than can be carried out with the limited facilities available in the community.

When a mental illness deprives the person of access to usual community services

Sometimes, the person with LD's mental illness or behavioural disorder can deprive them of access to 'normal' community facilities (e.g. violence or sexual disinhibition may make it unsafe for them to go to doctor's surgeries, shops, parks, college, etc.).

People with LD who are assessed as needing to be admitted to hospital may do so on a voluntary basis (i.e., they agree to it, and are admitted as an 'informal' patient), or they may refuse admission. If it is still thought by those responsible for them in the community that they need to go into hospital, in spite of their refusal, and that there is no safe alternative (or an alternative that will allow access to normal community facilities and a good quality of life) then a formal Mental Health Assessment is requested. In the UK this assessment has to be undertaken by an Approved Mental Health Professional – AMHP (formerly an 'Approved Social Worker'), a Psychiatrist approved under the Mental Health Act (Section 12-approved) and another Section 12-Approved Doctor, who may be a GP.

The professionals conducting the Mental Health Assessment have the power to enact:

- Section 2, a hospital assessment order (which may also involve treatment), which lasts for 28 days, or

- Section 3, a hospital treatment order, which lasts for up to 6 months (Section 3, but not section 2, may be renewed).

They also have the power to convey the person with LD to the hospital. If the diagnosis is unknown, Section 2 is usually appropriate, and, if known, Section 3 is the most suitable. In the UK, people with LD, like other people with mental disorders who are detained in hospital under the Mental Health Act, have the right to appeal against their detention. He or she can appeal at any time to the hospital managers, who have the right to discharge them from detention, irrespective of the Responsible Clinician's wishes. They may also appeal to the Mental Health Review Tribunal (under Section 2, within first 14 days, Section 3 during first 6 months of detention) who have powers equivalent to a court and who likewise can discharge people from detention.

When the person with LD has been involved in a crime

In such cases, court orders may dictate that the person be assessed in hospital for a report to the court, or be remanded to hospital for treatment. There is different law in different countries. In the UK attempts are usually made, using special provisions in the Mental Health Act 1983, to divert offenders with mental illness and/or learning disability away from the criminal justice system, but this is a very complex area.

There are offenders who, because of their intellectual limitations, or due to the effects of a mental illness, lack the necessary mental capacity to even appear in court. Taken into account here are such things as their ability to:

- understand the nature of the charges against them
- retain that information
- use the information in formulating their defence
- instruct legal counsel (solicitor)
- retain the information
- make decisions and remember them
- cross-examine a witness, and
- clearly convey their decisions to others.

In this area, the Mental Capacity Act 2005 is employed (see section on capacity, Chapter 6). If the person with LD is thought to lack the necessary mental capacity to appear in court, the court may request a formal Mental Capacity Assessment. If this confirms their suspicions, the court may decide to order the person with LD to go into hospital for 28 days for a report, under Section 35 of the Mental Health Act.

Other people with LD who have an established history of mental illness may also come before the courts in connection with charges against them. These people, too, may lack mental capacity to appear in court. The court may decide that, as the diagnosis is known, an assessment order is not required, and they may then order the person with LD to be treated in hospital under Section 37 of the Mental Health Act 2007 (a 6-month order).

Some people with LD may appear in court, having not been assessed as unfit to appear due to lack of capacity, but it may become apparent to the court that they are not following the procedure of the court or making themselves understood, or are unable to communicate properly. In such a case, the court may order an independent psychiatric report from a psychiatrist ('expert report'). On the basis of this report, the courts in the UK may, if they so decide, remand the person with LD to hospital for a further (hospital) report (Section 35), or remand the person with LD to hospital for treatment (Section 37).

Sometimes, the person with LD may have been sentenced to a prison term, and the prison doctors are so concerned about their mental health, that they refer the person to a hospital for treatment and/or assessment.

Hospital care and standards

When such a person with LD is admitted to hospital, the carer(s) should make an appointment to see the 'Named Nurse' (a nurse who takes the lead in organising someone's care), to discuss any concerns they may have, and to impart any information that they may think will assist the hospital staff in assessing or treating the person with LD. The hospital has a duty to provide a written care plan for the person with LD in hospital, whether detained or not, he or she has the right of access to advocacy services, and to a solicitor of his or her choice.

Carers are encouraged to keep in contact with the hospital and with the person with LD. Where appropriate, and with the person's consent, they may attend clinical review meetings, as may advocates from the advocacy services. These multi professional meetings, sometimes called Care Programme Approach (CPA) meetings, review care plans, risk assessments, agree leave outside the hospital and all aspects of care leading to and including discharge planning.

Hospitals in the UK operate under strict laws, and have to follow detailed, legally enforceable policies and procedures in respect of every aspect of care, which have been agreed with the Care Quality Commission in England, Wales and Northern Ireland. The principal laws are listed in Box 13.1. The Royal College of Psychiatrists has produced some quality standards for LD and other mental health inpatient units (Accreditation for Inpatient Mental health Services (AIMS)-LD) that address these issues and have been taken up by many units across the country.

Box 13.1 Principal laws underlying hospital policy in the UK

- The Mental Health Act 1983 amended 2007
- The Mental Capacity Act 2005 (includes Deprivation of Liberty Safeguards – DOLS)
- The Human Rights Act 1998
- Criminal Justice Act 2003 (allows transfer of prisoners to hospital for care)
- Disability Discrimination Act 1995, extended 2005
- Care Standards Act 2000
- Common Law

Clearly, because of the very great volumes of law that determine the appropriateness of all aspects of a person with LDs care, assessment, treatment, rights, etc., and upon which hospital policies are based, a small handbook like this cannot deal with the subject in great detail.

People who have caring roles for people with LDs are best advised to seek clarification and explanation about any matter of concern to them with the person with LDs named nurse, the responsible clinician or the hospital managers. If the person with LD consents, they may also attend manager's review meetings, and/ or mental health review tribunals, where they will also be able to state their concerns, if any. Sometimes the advocate of the person with LD may also be able to assist carers or relatives in respect of things they don't know or understand.

Finally, it should be remembered that being admitted to hospital is a 'last-resort' option for people with LD, and that if they are admitted, the entire focus and intention of the care plan devised for (and, where possible, with) them should have as its main goal a speedy return to living in the least restrictive possible community setting. The community mental health service members who were involved with the person with LD before admission should remain involved, attend the multi-disciplinary ward meetings and contribute to the care plan. The person will be returning to their care, and so they should not have lost contact with them.

Hospitals also have duties to keep the person with LD's GP, community psychiatrist and other members of the community mental health team up to date with what is happening, the person's progress and what plans are being made for discharge. They do this by means of regular reports during the course of an admission, and, at the time of discharge, by sending a detailed discharge report. If a person is detained under section 3, or an equivalent section, there is special provision within the MHA (section 117 after care) to ensure appropriate resources and care support is available on discharge at no extra expense to the person; for example if a person needs an extra waking staff member to reduce the risk of harm.

Appendix
Genetic causes of learning disability

Genetics is the science of heredity (the passing of traits to offspring from parents/ancestors), and inherited variation in living organisms. In recent years the science of genetics has moved forward rapidly. New tests become available regularly, and, with these, more and more subtle genetic changes can be identified as possible causes of learning disability and many other conditions. In this appendix we will very briefly explain some of the basics of genetics, and then look at some genetic conditions causing learning disability and their impact on the way in which people might behave and why they might lead to specific health problems.

The conditions described in this appendix are only a sample of the many genetic disorders that exist, but we hope that it is useful in providing an overview of some of the main genetic disorders and giving some indication of how the needs of people with learning difficulties will differ depending upon the nature of their condition.

Remember, you should always consult an expert in genetics if the person with LD you are caring for is thought to have a genetic abnormality because, as this appendix will make clear, genetics is a complicated field of expertise.

Introducing the basics of genetics

The basic building block of genetics is DNA (which is the abbreviation of deoxyribonucleic acid). This comprises two long chains of sugar bases (nucleotides) wrapped around each other in a shape commonly known as a 'double helix'. Figure A.1 shows a simple drawing of a double helix.

Figure A.1 The double helix of DNA in a chromosome

There are four nucleotide bases, Adenine (A), Guanine (G), Cytosine (C) and Thymine (T), specific combinations of which – of a certain length and in a certain place – are called 'genes'. They determine codes for the production of proteins that eventually make us into what we are, and ensure our bodies function properly. DNA is carried on chromosomes (from the Greek *Chromo* – colour and *Soma* – body).

Chromosomes look like two strings of pearls attached in one place by a knot (centromere), as shown in Figure A.2.

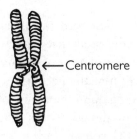

Figure A.2 Chromosomes

On chromosomes there are two short arms (P) and two long arms (Q). In humans there are 46 chromosomes of different shapes and sizes (this is called a 'karyotype'). Normally there are 23 pairs of chromosomes, one from each of the parents. One of these pairs defines the sex of a person; this pair is called the X and Y chromosomes or 'sex-chromosomes': a pair of XX = female, a pair comprising X and Y =

male. The other chromosomes (numbered 1 to 22) are present in both males and females and are called 'autosomes' (see Figure A.3).

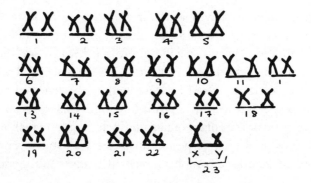

Figure A.3 The 23 paired chromosomes of the human male

The process by which a sperm (from the male) and egg/ovum (from the female) carry the chromosomes and eventually develop into a person is an extremely complex process, and cannot be covered in detail here. Suffice to say, this process involves a series of intricate divisions of the chromosomes, along with the manufacture of a large range of proteins from the huge number of genes that are coded for on the chromosomes.

Given the complexity of these processes, it is not surprising that problems can arise within genes and chromosomes. If the problems are small, then no ill-effects are likely to occur in the development of the foetus. However, if certain critical defects occur, then quite marked abnormal development can result. With respect to learning disability (LD), these abnormalities may be seen early on in life. Other genetic conditions that are not associated with learning disabilities may only become apparent much later in life – for example, Huntington's Chorea and certain cancers.

The most common genetic problems are:

- abnormalities with the number of sex chromosomes or other non-sex chromosomes – autosomes ('Aneuploidies') – with there being too few or too many

- chromosomes breaking – segments may be lost ('deletions'), pieces may detach and re-attach in the wrong direction ('inversion'), sections may be included twice ('duplications') and two different pairs of chromosomes may swap segments ('translocations').

There are many different tests for abnormal chromosome numbers or structure. Some are easier to identify then others. However, it is helpful to know what a specific disorder is because specific health or personality or behavioural problems may be associated with it. The latter two of these are often described as 'behavioural phenotypes' – 'phenotype' is a technical term, but simply refers to an observable characteristic or trait of an organism (including humans). An example of a behavioural phenotype might be the voracious over-eating, self injury and emotional problems seen in Prader Willi Syndrome (see later).

Another reason to try and find the cause of LD is to identify hereditary problems that can be passed down through a family. In such cases, it can be useful to know about future risk before a family member has a child. However, other genetic conditions may arise spontaneously, without extra risk in future pregnancies.

The risk of inheriting a genetic disorder depends on a number of factors:

- *dominant conditions* (there are over 40 linked with LD): these only need one abnormal chromosome from either parent. The risk is 50 per cent in future births from the same parents.

- *recessive conditions* (5 per cent of all births) require one abnormal chromosome from both parents. Risk increased if parents closely related. There are over 130 known conditions linked to LD.

- *sex-linked conditions* (passed on via the X chromosome). The problems here are more likely to be seen in males, as they have no second X chromosome to 'balance' the abnormality.

Signs and symptoms in an affected person that could suggest a genetic problem

Clusters of abnormal body structure ('dysmorphology') may be seen. These can be external (e.g. cleft lip, unusual facial features, missing digits, etc.) or internal (e.g. heart abnormalities, organs in the wrong place). There may be a family history of a certain condition (e.g. learning disability) or specific characteristic behaviours displayed by a person – a behavioural phenotype, as explained above.

In order to establish whether or not someone with developmental delay has a genetic problem paediatricians and GP's may refer to a clinical geneticist (often based in regional centres). They can arrange more detailed physical examinations, to investigate the family tree, and to arrange counselling prior to any blood tests. Specific blood tests or other investigations may then be arranged. Many regional centres will retain frozen blood samples (with consent) to allow further testing as new tests become available and new genetic conditions are identified. After diagnosis they offer support and advice about management of conditions and risks to subsequent pregnancies and to other family members should they become pregnant.

Common genetic conditions

Below we provide a brief explanation of some genetic conditions that cause LD, grouped by the way in which the chromosome strucure is affected. Although this list is far from complete, it gives an idea of the range of conditions that are seen within the population that have LD.

Too many chromosomes

The severity of these conditions depends on how many cells have abnormal numbers of chromosomes. In 'full forms' of these conditions every cell is affected and the person may show the most severe aspects of the disorder. In 'mosaic forms' only some cells have the abnormal number of chromosomes and the person may show fewer aspects. In 'partial forms' there may be an extra copy of part of the chromosome. Though the clinical features and consequent disability shown may be less severe, there may be hereditary risks in future pregnancies.

TOO MANY AUTOSOMES

- Down's syndrome (three chromosome 'trisomy 21') is the commonest genetic condition in people with learning disabilities, and for this reason we discussed its associated health problems in more detail earlier in this book. The condition occurs because of abnormalities in chromorosme 21. There are three types of abnormality:

- *non-dysjunction*, when chromosomal material fails to separate in the egg, which happens in most cases (95 per cent). This is a non-inherited problem, which can be related to factors such as increasing parental age, or which can just be spontaneous.

- *mosaicism*, where not all cells have three chromosomes. This happens in 1 per cent of people with Down's syndrome. People may be less affected (particularly in terms of intelligence and skills).

- *translocation*, where chromosomal material is rearranged in all cells; this occurs in 4 per cent.

The presence of the last two conditions increases the risk of a further child being born with Down's syndrome. This risk can also be increased for other family members who decide to have children. Genetic testing can differentiate between the types of condition a potential parent might be subject to, and can be used to give appropriate counselling and advice.

The birth rate of babies with Down's syndrome nowadays appears to be fairly stable (being approximately one per thousand live births).

Since physical and mental health problems increase with age, it is important that carers are aware of potential health problems in those they care for. Regular health checks may pick up problems early on, and thereby improve outcomes.

- *Edward's syndrome* (three chromosomes, 'trisomy' 18) – Seen in approximately 3 births per 10,000, the full form of this condition is associated with severe disability and low survival rates beyond the first years of life. However, people with 'mosaic' or 'partial' trisomy may have milder forms of learning disability and improved life expectancy. Features include growth retardation, clenched hands, low-set/malformed ears, heart defects and breathing difficulties.

- *Patau's syndrome* ('trisomy' 13) – Seen in approximately 2 births per 10,000, it is associated with severe learning disability. Physical characteristics include low birth weight, heart defects, eye problems, cleft palate and spinal cord defects. There may be abdominal defects and abnormal genitalia. On the hands there can be abnormal palm patterns, extra digits and fingers overlapping the thumb. Those with the full form of the disorder may have low survival rates beyond early childhood.

TOO MANY SEX CHROMOSOMES

- *Klinefelter's syndrome* – This syndrome occurs only in males, and is due to having too many X chromosomes. Though usually a spontaneous mutatuion, risk may be increased with older mothers. It can be associated with milder forms of learning disability and a number of physical features, including small testes, sterility, lack of body hair and breast development (after puberty), and a 'gynaecoid habitus' (or feminine body-shape). Some psychological problems may be reported, including passivity, apprehensiveness, shyness, difficulties making relationships, possibly related to issues with body image, etc. Some aspects may respond to the use of supplementary hormones (testosterone).

- *XYY syndrome* ('Super-Male') – this occurs in 1 per 1,000 males. There are a number of similarities with Klinefelter's syndrome, though there may be more assertiveness and restless impulsivity, with a degree of immature personality.

Too few chromosomes

TOO FEW AUTOSOMES

- In general the complete loss of an autosome proves fatal early in development. Up to 40 per cent of conceptions will abort spontaneously during pregnancy, and much of this loss is due to major chromosomal abnormality.

TOO FEW SEX CHROMOSOMES

- *Turner's syndrome* (XO) – This is one of the most common chromosome disorders, affecting 1 in 250 girls. Characteristic features include short stature, general absence of pubertal development, non-functioning ovaries and subsequent infertility. There may be webbing of the neck, wide-spaced nipples and small hands/feet. Some abnormalities of the main blood vessels may also occur. Generally, girls with Turner's syndrome have an IQ in the normal range, but mild disability may occur. There may be some cognitive problems (e.g. weaker verbal reasoning and memory skills). There may be problems with peer relationships, resulting in shyness and social anxiety.

Mutations on sex chromosomes

- *Rett's syndrome* – This condition, carried on the X chromosome, is seen almost only in females, possibly due to the fact there are no compensating X chromosomes in males, which increases the death rate of male babies. It affects 1 in every 12,500 female live births. Children born with Rett's syndrome often show normal development until the age of 6 to 12 months. After that there is slowed head growth, an 'autistic-like' withdrawal, often with screaming fits, panic attacks, crying and general lack of interest, plus avoidance of social interaction. Balance and coordination problems may develop with repetitive movements (particularly with mid-line hand wringing), seizures and breathing irregularities (including hyperventilation and breath-holding). Cognitive decline and muscular skeletal problems occur (dystonia and spasticity, as seen in cerebral palsy), which go on to cause severe learning and physical disabilities.

- *Fragile X syndrome (FRAX)* – This is the most commonly identified form of inherited learning disability, affecting about 1 in 4,000 males and 1 in 8,000 females. It is caused by over-expansion of a single series of three nuclear type bases (CGG) at the end of an X chromosome. Because males have no other balancing X chromosome, symptoms of this condition are more prominent in boys. Characteristics include an elongated face, large protruding ears, larger testes ('macro-orchidism'), poor muscle tone and oddities in speech. Behaviours such as stereotyped movements (e.g. hand flapping), and abnormal social development (particularly shyness, limited eye contact and autistic-like problems) may be seen. A number will also meet the criteria for a full diagnosis of autism. Affected people often have relaxed ligaments and this may cause hyper-extension of joints and problems with the valves of the heart.

• *Lesch-Nyhan syndrome* – this is an X-linked recessive disorder, usually carried by the mother and passed on to her son. One third of cases may be derived from new mutations, the others showing a family history. The condition is mainly seen in boys, with only a few rare cases of affected females. The mutation occurs in about 1 in 380,000 live births. The gene mutation causes problems with an enzyme, which leads to a build up of uric acid in body fluids. Children will then suffer motor delays and muscular problems – for example, developing spasms and jerky movements. Learning disability is variable, but often moderate to severe. Behavioural disturbances are common, the most striking feature being compulsive self-injurious behaviour, with biting of the lips, the inside of the mouth and tongue, and all fingers being common. Restraint is sometimes required to limit the physical trauma. Significant health problems include kidney damage from the excess uric acid, as well as gout (inflammation of joints by uric acid).

Partial loss of chromosomes (Deletions)

These occur when part of the chromosomes' genetic material is missing. The missing pieces may contain important genes, without which the body and brain may develop differently. Examples include the following:

• *Prader-Willi syndrome (PWS)* – This condition may affect 1 in 22,000 births, and is due to loss of material from the father's chromosome 15. Symptoms include babies who are floppy (due to low muscle tone), and who then grow up to have immature development of sexual organs, excessive appetite with over-eating, growth and sex hormone dysfunction, short stature, emotional problems and varying degrees of learning disability. Some people with this syndrome may develop a psychotic mental illness during adolescence. Some people may benefit from hormone supplements, to help their growth and sexual development. The majority of health risks for people with PWS are linked to obesity. It is vital to help the person to manage their diet and weight, particularly if the person has significant learning disability and lacks capacity to make choices. This type of help may first be accessed through the local community learning disability services. In extreme circumstances specialist residential services are available for this client group. Best-interests decisions will need to be taken by professionals and carers to minimise the health risks of unrestricted food intake, such as fitting locks to fridges or cupboards.

- *Angelman syndrome* (AS) – This condition affects about 1 in 20,000 births and is due to the loss of material from the mother's chromosome 15. Features include severe learning disability, minimal speech development, movement and balance disorders (ataxia), behaviour that includes frequent laughing/smiling, an excitable personality and body movements such as hand flapping. A major health problem is epilepsy, seen in more than 80 per cent of people with this condition. This can be sometimes difficult to treat. Physiotherapy is often important to prevent stiffening of joints and loss of movement. Many people with AS have limited sleep and can be quite overactive and have a short attention span.

- *Smith-Magenis syndrome* – This condition affects approximately 1 in 25,000 births. It is due to loss of material from chromosome 17. Features include changes to facial appearance and disrupted sleep patterns. Many will have behavioural problems, including frequent temper tantrums, anxiety, impulsiveness and problems with attention. Self-injurious behaviour is common, and may include biting, head-banging and skin-picking. People may often self-hug (possibly to reduce self-injury). Physical features also include short stature, abnormal curvature of the spine (sclerosis), reduced sensitivity to pain and temperature, and problems with poor hearing. Medication may be helpful in improving sleep/wake pattern. Melatonin (a hormone connected to sleep) can be useful – see Chapter 8 of this book.

Other genetic disorders

- *Tuberous sclerosis (TS)* – This condition is seen in approximately in 1 to 1.5 per 10,000 births. It is an autosomal-dominant condition linked to mutations on chromosomes 9 and 16. In affected individuals the body is unable to control cell growth very well. As a consequence a number of lesions ('tubers') develop in many parts of the body, including the brain, kidneys, heart, lungs, eyes and skin. The tubers can result in a number of health conditions, including epilepsy (which can be difficult to treat), kidney dysfunction, learning disability and heart problems. Regular health-monitoring, including CT brain scans, ultrasounds of the heart and kidneys, eye checks, etc., are recommended. Tubers may increase in size, may bleed or, rarely, turn malignant. There are a number of warning signs that warrant rapid investigations, including increased seizure frequency, blood in the urine and severe abdominal pain. Carers should be aware of potential problems in order to manage risks better.

Glossary

abdominal aortic aneurysm – abnormal enlargement of the main artery in the body

adaptive intelligence – the way in which the human mind will tend to change (adapt) in an environment toward more positive modes of functioning

adjunctive treatment – extra, or secondary, treatment

adjustment disorder – mental disorder following traumatic events

advocacy – support or argument for a cause (the person doing this is the 'advocate')

aerobic – requiring oxygen

affective disorder – mental disorder in which mood is predominantly affected

alexia – inability to 'see' words or to read

Alzheimer's disease – a degenerative illness in which cognitive abilities and skills are lost over time

amino acids – the chemical compounds that are the building blocks of proteins

anaemia – a group of conditions in which the blood has a reduced ability to carry oxygen

anaerobic – not requiring oxygen

aneuploides – abnormal number of chromosomes

angina (*pectoris*) – chest pains on exercise (due to **ischemia** of heart muscle)

antecedent – coming before, and contributing to something

anticholinesterase inhibitors – drugs that increase the levels of chemicals in the brain, to help treat dementia

aortic aneurysm – 'ballooning' of the main blood vessel in the body

aortic stenosis – narrowing of the main 'outflow' valve of the heart

aplastic anaemia – anaemia due to inability of bone marrow to produce red blood cells

apnoea – cessation of breathing (temporary)

Arnold-Chiari malformation – an abnormality of the brain where a particular part (the cerebellar tonsils) is pushed down through the opening at the base of the skull, sometimes causing an increase in fluid pressure (hydrocephalus)

arrhythmia – abnormal heart rhythm (seen on an electrocardiograph (ECG))

arterial walls – the walls of the arteries, the blood vessels which carry blood away from the heart to the rest of the body

arteriosclerosis – hardening of the arteries by fatty materials, which become calcified

atheroma – deposition of fatty material in arterial wall

atonic seizure – epileptic fit, causing loss of muscle tone

autism – a disorder with strict and standardised criteria first recognised in childhood resulting in problems with communication, social interaction and repetitive behaviours

autistic spectrum disorder – not all people with autism are the same. There is a range from severe conditions, with limited abilities and significant LD, to normal intelligence and high levels of functioning. All are associated with degrees of impairment in communication, social interaction and behaviour

autosomal – relating to an autosome, i.e. a chromosome that is not a sex chromosome

autosome – non-sex chromosome

barrier cream – cream to protect the skin

behavioural phenotype – a set of behaviours associated with some inherited disorders

benzodiazepine – a class of drugs that treat anxiety, insomnia or epilepsy

best interest principle – an attitude that puts the best interest of a person who lacks capacity at the centre of any decision making process about them

biopsy – taking a tissue sample from the body for analysis

bipolar affective disorder – mood disorder in which high or low moods can occur

birth anoxia – lack of oxygen to the body at the time of birth

blepharitis – infection/inflammation of eyelid

blood oxygen saturation – the amount of oxygen the blood is carrying, which falls if there are problems with the heart and lungs

Body Mass Index (BMI) – a measure that includes weight and height, by which it is calculated whether someone has an appropriate, excessive or insufficient weight

buccal – inside the mouth

caffeine – a stimulant compound found in tea, coffee and Coca-Cola

cardiac ischaemia – lack of blood to the heart, usually caused by narrowed arteries

cardiovascular reserve – the ability of the heart to cope with the extra demand for blood associated with exercise

carotene – a form of vitamin A

cataract – opacity and 'milkiness' of the eye lens, leading to defective vision

central nervous system – the brain and spinal cord

centromere – the point at which two paired chromosomes are joined

cerebral malaria – a malarial infection of the brain which can cause significant brain damage and is sometimes fatal

cerebral palsy – perinatal brain damage

cerebrovascular disease – refers to conditions or diseases of the heart and blood vessels including coronary artery disease (blocked arteries in the heart), angina (pain in the chest on exercise, heart failure, high blood pressure and strokes

chromosome – long strands of genetic material, which occur in pairs within cells

clubbing – unusually shaped nails, often associated with low oxygen levels in the blood, which can be caused by a number of long-term health problems

cluster seizures – several epileptic seizures happening in a short space of time

coffee ground vomit – vomit that looks like used coffee grounds and which suggests bleeding stomach

common law – law developed by judges through past decisions of courts and tribunals rather than through legislative statute

co-morbid – more than one pathology occurring together at the same time

congenital – something somebody is born with

congestive cardiac failure – heart failure in which the organs become congested due to 'pump' failure of the heart

contra-indication – a reason why a medication should not be used

cornea – outer covering of the eye

cretinism – outdated term for somebody suffering learning disabilities due to infantile hypothyroidism

CT scan – computerised tomography scan

cyanosis – a bluish colour of lips or extremities caused by heart or lung problems

cytomegalovirus – a viral infection which is usually mild in adults but which can cause problems (including learning disability and sensory problems) to an unborn baby if the mother is infected

deletion (chromosomal) – a loss of some of the genetic material on a chromosome

delusion – a demonstrably false belief, held against evidence to the contrary

dementia – a disorder leading to loss of cognitive functions

deoxyribonucleic acid (DNA) – the chemical structure that comprises the genes

depression – a condition in which lowered mood is a central feature

desultory thinking – a formal thought disorder in which normal-sounding phrases or sentences are inappropriately juxtaposed

detruser instability – the muscular wall of the bladder contracting too soon

development milestone – age at which children can carry out specific tasks, e.g. walk, say single words

differential diagnosis – a method of diagnosis that involves determining which of a variety of possible candidates is the probable cause of an individuals symptoms, often by a process of elimination

disinhibition – reduced ability to manage an impulsive response to a situation

dominant condition – an inherited condition in which only one chromosome is needed from one parent to have the disorder/characteristic

drop attack – (see also atonic seizure) epileptic seizure leading to falling as a result of loss of muscle tone. Also known as an akinetic attack

dyslexia – difficulty 'seeing' words, or reading

dysmenorrhoea – painful periods

dysmorphology – abnormal appearance or structure of body, or body part

dyspepsia – indigestion

dysphagia – difficulty swallowing

dyspnoea – shortness of breath

dysuria – pain on passing water

echocardiogram – a test using ultrasound to show the structure and functions of the heart

echolalia – repetition of a word or phrase by a person

electroconvulsive therapy – a type of treatment for severe psychiatric illness, e.g. depression not responding to other treatment

electroencephalogram – a reading of the electrical waves of the brain

encephalitis – infection of the brain

endocrine – relating to the function of glands that secrete hormones inside the body (e.g. the thyroid gland)

epistatus – a trade name of a medicine (Midozolam) used for stopping of an epileptic seizure

evidence-based – shown to be of benefit through scientific evaluation published in reliable journals

extra pyramidal – the extrapyramidal system is a network of motor nerves in the brain, which help to coordinate movement. In this instance referring to side-effects of drugs characterised by tremor and stiffness

febrile convulsion – seizure occurring in a child with a temperature

food groups – the major categories of food broken down into the main types of nutrients they contain for example: protein, carbohydrates; fats and sugar; meat and vegetable protein; fruit and vegetables; milk and dairy products

Fragile X syndrome – where there is a mutated site on the X chromosome, which can result in learning disability and certain behavioural and health characteristics

generalisation (of a seizure) – process where epileptic activity starting in one place in the brain spreads to involve the whole brain

genetic (gene) – a feature coded for by sequences of nucleotide bases in the **DNA**

genetic syndromes – the physical, psychological and behavioural results of abnormalities in genetic make up

gluconeogenesis – metabolic process in which glucose is produced from non-carbohydrate sources (e.g. protein)

glycogen – a carbohydrate storage compound: the compound the body mainly stores its sugars in

gynaecoid habitus – body morphology that looks female (even if it is male)

haematuria – the presence of blood in the urine

haemoptysis – coughing up blood

hallucination – experiencing the presence of something that is not there (visual, auditory, tactile, etc.)

hepatitis B – a viral infection that can damage the liver

heredity – process by which characteristics are inherited from one generation to the next

hernia – displacement and protrusion of part of an organ through the wall of the cavity containing it

hydrocephalus, hydrocephaly – abnormal amount of fluid within the brain

hyper-extension – when the joint is over-extended, which can lead to pain or other problems

hypermetropia – long sightedness

hypertension – an abnormally high blood pressure, over a period of time. Can damage body systems leading to complications like stroke and heart attack

hyperthyroidism – condition due to abnormally high thyroid hormone levels in the body

hypnotic (medication) – a drug used to induce sleep

hypoglycaemic drugs – drugs that lower glucose, used to treat diabetes

hypomania – pathologically elevated mood state, without delusions

hypothyroidism – a condition where there is low levels of the hormone thyroxin, due to an underactive thyroid gland

hypoxia – low blood oxygen levels

ictal – relating to an epileptic seizure or fit. NB also periods before a fit (pre-ictal) and after (post-ictal)

infarction – tissue death due to lack of sufficient oxygenated blood supply (e.g. myocardial infarction – heart attack)

insomnia – difficulty sleeping

intravenous – into a vein

inversion (genetic) – process by which pieces of a chromosome may be abnormally changed around

iodine – an element essential for the production of thyroxine

ischemia – lack of sufficient oxygenated blood supply to a tissue (e.g. myocardial ischemia – angina)

karyotype – the number and appearance of chromosomes in the nucleus of a cell the genetic arrangement responsible for a physical phenotype

keratoconus – protruding cornea

labelling – society's negative and unhelpful way of ascribing names to people who are different

laceration – a serious cut

lactic acid – a chemical that builds up in muscles when not enough oxygen is present

Lennox Gastaut syndrome – a type of epilepsy with lots of seizure types

leukaemia – a malignancy affecting white blood cells

macro-orchidism – large testicles

Makaton – a sign language used by some people who have no speech (e.g. deaf people)

mammography – an X-ray screening test to look for breast cancer

mania – pathologically elevated mood-state with delusions

melaena – black, tar-like diarrhoea, caused by bleeding in the gut

Melatonin – naturally occurring hormone involved in sleep regulation

meningitis – infection of the meninges or lining of the brain

metabolic disorder – disorder of the chemical processes in the body that produce energy

mid-line hand wringing – wringing of the hands while holding them in the middle of the body

monotherapy – the use of a single drug to treat a condition (e.g. epilepsy)

morbidity – an incidence of ill health

mosaic (mosaicism) – a condition where some cells have abnormal chromosome or genetic content, but not all

MRI scan (Magnetic Resonance Imaging Scan) – sophisticated computerised scan of body or parts of body, using the magnetic properties of water contained in cells

MSU – mid-stream urine sample (to ensure its sterility)

mucopolysaccharidosis – an inherited disorder in the synthesis of important sugars

myocardial infarction – a blockage of one of the heart's blood vessels, leading to death (necrosis) of part of the heart muscle (heart attack)

myopia – short sightedness

neologism – an invented word

neonatal period – the first 28 days following birth

neuroleptic – a drug affecting the central nervous system used in mental illness (also called an antipsychotic)

neurological – relating to the nervous system

neurone – a nerve cell

non-dysjunction – a failure of separation of two chromosomes during cell division

normal pressure hydrocephalus – a rare condition when excess fluid collects in the brain leading to unsteadiness

nucleotide base – a chemical that makes up the building blocks of **DNA**

obesity – being more than 15 per cent heavier than you should be for your height

obsessive – when one has repetitive, often distressing thoughts that are difficult to suppress

obstructive sleep apnoea – temporary cessation of breathing while asleep, due to obstruction in the airway, often causing wakening

oesophagitis – inflammation of the oesophagus

palpitations – conscious awareness of the heart beating, usually with 'increased' rate or force

parasthesia – abnormal sensations in skin, e.g. itching, 'crawling'

pathology – deviation from the healthy or normal condition, or studies into the effect of disease on the body

peg feed – Per-Endoscopic-Gastrostomy: a feeding tube inserted through the skin and abdominal wall, directly into the stomach

pericarditis – infection or inflammation of the outer lining membranes of the heart

peripheral vascular problems – narrowing of the arteries in the arms and legs leading to a poor blood supply

personality disorder – a disorder that is present from before adolescence, which continues throughout life, and which causes disruption or difficulty for the affected person as well as others, but is not due to mental illness or some other disorder

phenotype – physical appearance caused by a genotype

phenylketonuria – an autosomal dominant inherited disorder associated with learning disability

phobia – a pathological fear of an object or circumstance

placenta praevia – a condition where the placenta is attached to the uterine wall close to or covering the cervix

pleurisy – infection and/or inflammation of the lung lining

pneumonia – infection and congestion of the lungs

polycythaemia – an abnormally high red-blood-cell count

post ictally – referring to the period of time after a seizure

Post Traumatic Stress Disorder (PTSD) – psychological disorder arising from a trauma that is outside the normal range of human experience

poverty of thought – lack of normal amount of thinking, caused by chronic mental illness, severe learning disability or over-sedation

PR indicated – rectal examination indicated

Prader Willi syndrome – a complex genetic disorder present from birth characterised by an excessive appetite, emotional instability and learning disability

primary generalised seizure – a seizure immediately involving both halves of the brain with no warning

Primary Health Care Team – the staff team working in primary health care services, e.g. doctors, nurses and physiotherapists

psychosis – mental illness characterised by several features, but mainly where 'reality' is said to be lost

psychotropic drugs – drugs that act on the mind

PV discharge – vaginal discharge

recessive conditions (genetic) – inherited condition in which two abnormal genes, one from each parent, are required to produce the condition

rescue medication – urgent, extra medication used to control epileptic seizures that occur in spite of other anti-epileptic medication

rheumatoid arthritis – an inflammatory condition mainly affecting the joints, causing swelling, pain and reduced mobility

rubella – German measles. This is usually a mild viral illness in adults, but can cause serious problems (including learning disability, deafness and cataracts) to an unborn baby if the mother is infected

savant ability – an isolated, sometimes extremely complex, ability occurring in someone otherwise quite disabled (e.g. calendrical calculation ability in person with very low IQ)

scabies – parasitic infection of the skin

schizophasia – the disintegration of speech into a meaningless 'word salad'

secondary generalised seizures – when epileptic activity starts in one point of the brain, often giving rise to a warning sign, e.g. funny feelings in the stomach, before spreading across the brain to affect both sides

self-injurious behaviour – behaviour in which a person harms themselves (e.g. head-banging, self-cutting)

senna – a laxative

serial ability – to monitor someone's skills and cognitive function at intervals over time to ensure there is no deterioration. May be done if dementia is suspected

sex-linked conditions – inherited disorders carried on the X or Y ('sex') chromosomes

side-effects – any effect of a drug, other than that intended when prescribing it

softening laxative – medication used to soften the stool

somatoform disorder – psychological disorder in which physical symptoms are experienced

specific phobia – a phobia of a particular thing, e.g. spiders

status epilepticus – on-going seizure, difficult to stop

statute law – written law set down by a legislature

tachypnoea – fast breathing rate

talking therapies – treatment given by talking about problems or worries rather than by medication

tetanus – serious, life-threatening illness due to a bacterium that produces a toxin which affects the nervous system

thought blocking – experience of sudden cessation in the flow of one's thought

thought broadcast – experience of feeling one can transmit thoughts to someone else's brain

thought disorder – term used to describe a variety of abnormalities in the form of thought, which may occur in psychosis

thought insertion – experience of feeling someone else is transmitting thoughts to one's brain

thyroid gland – the gland in the neck that produces thyroid hormone

thyrotoxicosis – condition caused by an over-active thyroid gland

thyroxine – hormone produced by the thyroid gland

tonic-clonic – descriptive term for phases of a generalised seizure, in which the muscles are first tensed, and then react in a jerky way

toxoplasma – an infection caused by a parasite usually caught from cat faeces but also from uncooked meats

trace elements – important dietary substances that are needed in minute amounts

translocation – part of a chromosome being located in the wrong site

trisomy – having a third chromosome where there should only be two

tuberous sclerosis – an autosomal dominant inherited condition, associated with learning disability

tubers – small tumours occurring in the brain in **tuberous sclerosis**

word salad – impossible-to-understand speech, in which words are put together in a seemingly random and meaningless way

References

Moss, S.C., Prosser, H., Costello, H., Simpson, N., Patel, P., Rowe, S., Turner, S., and Hatton, C. (1998) 'Reliability and validity of the PAS-ADD Checklist for detecting psychiatric disorders in adults with intellectual disability.' *Journal of Intellectual Disability Research 42*, 173-183.

Prasher, Dr V. and Smith, B. (2002) *Down's Syndrome and Health Care.* Kidderminster: Bild Publications.

Prasher, Dr V. and Janicki, M. (2002) *Physical Health of Adults with Intellectual Disability.* Oxford: Blackwell Publications.

Useful Websites

For many people it is difficult to access information on specific health issues to do with learning disability from local libraries. It can be even more difficult to locate published articles in professional journals, medical text books and other publications in this field. For this reason, throughout this book, we have avoided citing individual text references. Instead we have listed a number of easily accessible websites (operational at the time of press) that offer further information about areas covered in the book.

Easy Read Information about health conditions and medicines

www.easyhealth.org.uk – Leaflets and videos on various aspects of health.

www.ld-medication.bham.ac.uk/ – User-friendly leaflets and MP3 downloads on medication.

www.intellectualdisability.info/ – Collaborative website between St George's hospital medical school and the Downs Association, covering many areas of health and care for PWLD.

www.rcpsych.ac.uk/publications/booksbeyondwords – Royal College of Psychiatrists site with a variety of picture books to facilitate communication with PWLD.

http://www.elfrida.com/publications.html – Publishes materials by people with learning difficulties, for people with learning difficulties and for people who work with them.

Images and advice for creating easy to read information

www.changepeople.co.uk – Health picture bank and other resources.

http://www.google.co.uk/ – Variety of pictures /line drawings and cartoons that can be downloaded.

www.easyinfo.org.uk/ – Website that provides information on how to create easy to read literature for PWLD.

Specific genetic conditions

http://www.downs-syndrome.org.uk/ – Useful information sheets and publications on Down's syndrome, plus support and advice.

http://www.cafamily.org.uk/index.php?section=861 – Provides advice and information about many genetic disorders causing LD and provides support to parents / carers of all disabled children.

http://www.autism.org.uk/ – National Autistic Society provide advice, support and information on most aspects of autism.

http://www.tuberous-sclerosis.org/ – Health Information, leaflets and support for Tuberous Sclerosis.

www.ndss.org – National Down Syndrome Society advocates for people with Down's, with useful information about the syndrome

http://www.dhg.org.uk/a – Down's heart group is a charity offering support and information relating to heart conditions associated with Down's Syndrome

Information about general health and welfare issues relating to PWLD

http://www.nhs.uk/Pages/HomePage.aspx – NHS Choices website with health information and advice

http://www.sepho.org.uk/viewResource.aspx?id=12117 – South East Regional Public Health Group information sheet about the extent of health problems in people with Learning Disabilities (PWLD).

www.mencap.org.uk/ – Charity supporting PWLD. Site contains useful information leaflets on all aspects of LD. Also support available.

http://www.valuingpeople.gov.uk – Valuing People Now team, Links you to your local LD partnership board and other useful resources for PWLD.

http://www.bild.org.uk/ – Website of the British institute of Learning Disability (a charity working for PWLD) has various publications relating to health (including the book by Prasher and Smith cited in Chapter 5).

Epilepsy information

http://www.ilae-epilepsy.org/ – International League Against Epilepsy website with detailed information including epilepsy classification.

http://www.epilepsy.org.uk/ – Epilepsy Action with information all many aspects of epilepsy.

http://www.epilepsysociety.org.uk – The National Society for Epilepsy with information and advice about epilepsy.

Mental health and capacity issues

www.publicguardian.gov uk/mca/code-of-practice.htm – Mental Capacity Act 2005 Code of practice (ISBN: 978 011 7037465) an easy to read guide to the MCA with lots of case examples.

http://www.mind.org.uk/news – Charitable organisation providing advice, information and support about many aspects of mental health.

www.rcpsych.ac.uk/ – Royal College of Psychiatrists website with public areas that contain information leaflets on mental health problems.

http://www.dh.gov.uk/en/Publicationsandstatistics/Publications/PublicationsPolicyAndGuidance/DH_084597 –Mental Heath Act (1983 revised 2008) code of practice.

http://www.dcsf.gov.uk/everychildmatters/ – Department for Children Schools and Families website with information about children's issues, including the Children's Act.

Index